EARTH SURVIVAL GUIDE

Go to
www.EarthSurvivalGuideBook.com
for Free Resources to
Help You Survive

EARTH SURVIVAL GUIDE

Why You are Probably from Another Planet
and
How to Survive This One

Carrie Hart

Copyright © 2016 by Carrie Hart

All rights reserved. No part of this book may be reproduced or transmitted in any form or by any means, electronic or mechanical, including photocopying, recording, or by any information storage and retrieval system, without permission in writing from the publisher.

Published by Hart Enterprise Media,
a division of Systematique, Inc.

Printed in the United States of America

*To the wonderful i-am-this.com members who join me
at dawn to bring Spirit into our lives and the world.
Your love, thoughtfulness and support
have made this book possible.*

∞

*And, of course, to my husband, Ed, who has had the
tenacity to live with me and love me for forty years,
for which I am deeply grateful.*

Contents

Part I

1 Why You are Probably from Another Planet   3
2 How to Spot an Earthling   5
3 How We Got Here   15
4 Glossary of Some Earth Terms and Concepts   19

Part II

5 How to Survive (Even Thrive) on Earth   53
6 The Extraordinary Thing That Happened   57
7 The Planet of Ur   59
8 Earth and the Land of Ur   63
9 Humans Join in the Fun   69
10 How Power Animals Came to Be   75
11 Oscar Appears   81
12 What I Know About You   87
13 Oscar and Carrie Get to Work   91
14 Separate Mind   101
15 Flutterby Teaches Me to Reach Silence   107
16 Power Animals Revisited   113
17 Carrie's Vision   117
18 Inviting Power Animal Archetypes   123

19	How to Breathe Down	125
20	Power Animal Team	127
21	Power Animal Retrieval	137
22	Intuition	143
23	Spirit Songs	153
24	It's All About You	157

About the Author	161

PART I

Why You are Probably from Another Planet

1
Why You are Probably from Another Planet

For years, I have asked myself why some people seem so comfortable here (call them Earthlings) and others of us just wander about, not understanding what is going on, in a state of continual confusion.

Now, finally, I have come to an irrefutable conclusion: I am from another planet. I am from a place where they do things quite differently.

Further, I have noticed beings from a variety of planets. None of us fit in here on Earth, that's clear, but the ways in which we don't fit in are often very different.

To help all of the People from Other Planets (call them POPs)—and there are many, many of us--I have put together an Earth Survival Guide. It contains:

- How to Spot an Earthling
- How We Got Here

- A Glossary of Some Earth Terms and Concepts
- How to Survive on Earth.

And by the way, if you're not instantly and intuitively convinced that we descend from various planets, please answer this. Where do you think those odd names for drugs come from? Tylenol, Valium, Prozac, Viagra and Lyrica? These are not Earth words and the effect on the Earth body appears to be largely unknown to those who dispense them.

But most importantly, if some of us were not from other planets, why would apparently intelligent people, do such stupid things? Why would we, for example, get fat and debt-ridden and undermine the very things we desire? Because we're not from around here, that's why.

But now that we've found each other, I think we can pull together and make it through this Earth life alive. This Survival Guide is here to help you do just that.

2
How to Spot an Earthling

Earthlings are very easy to spot. They're the ones who get by so easily, who seem to naturally understand how things work here. And if they also have Earthling parents who taught them how to navigate Earth society, there's just no stopping them.

It's important to know who is an Earthling, because there are a few characteristics that make them very dangerous to POPs.

Here are a few tell-tale signs that someone may be an Earthling.

1. Earthlings "Get" Cause and Effect

Here are some giveaway statements you might hear from an Earthling:

"No dessert for me, I don't want to gain weight."

"I decided not to buy that big flat-screen TV. I'm saving for my children's college and our retirement in the Bahamas"

> "No wine for me. I'm the designated driver."

> "I go to the gym at 5 AM every day to make sure I'm not late for work."

These are examples of their belief in a concept called Cause and Effect, where what you do today causes certain things to happen in the future.

This is quite different from my planet, where I do whatever I like and then I just mentally project the circumstances and environment around me. The Earthling concept of watching carefully what you do right now in order to create something in the distant future seems so restrictive! Is that really how things work here?

But not only do they seem to understand Cause and Effect, they also get when it doesn't work. Listen:

> "I wouldn't waste my money on a lottery ticket. The odds are too great."

What does that mean? Are they saying that I'm not likely to win $10 million dollars? Why not? I paid my $2. I just don't get it.

2. Earthlings Practice Delayed Gratification

Delayed Gratification is a really odd Earth concept that seems highly related to the Cause and Effect approach.

With delayed gratification, you say no to something now so that you can say yes to something even better later. For example, instead of buying candy now, an Earthling child might be taught to save her money in order to get a beautiful doll later.

On my planet, since everything can be instantly created from your thoughts, there would be no purpose whatsoever in not eating the candy right now, since you could think the doll into being whenever you want. I think that's better, don't you?

3. Earthlings Seem to Like People

This one is so odd. Earthlings seem to like to gather together in large groups and make a lot of noise — and they find it energizing. They don't have to spend a day recovering from a party. And they don't seem to suffer during the party either. There's something called "small talk" that they enjoy, where they just say a lot of meaningless words and feel that they are "building" something called a Relationship.

Some Earthlings have created a ritual they call Networking, which is meant to foster Business Relationships. They gather together in a large room and exchange pieces of paper that are meant to visually express their Brand. While exchanging these cards, they take turns describing who they are and what they do in fewer than 30 seconds. Some think that the Brand must be conveyed in under 10 seconds, because that's all the time anyone has.

And if you're caught in an elevator with one of them, watch out! They have something they call an Elevator Speech, and it can be deadly!

And after the networking, they go through the cards, key the information into computers and send each other emails, with the intention of engaging each other in the earning, spending and exchanging of Money.

Building Relationships is very strange to POPs. On my planet, where there is no business and no money, we just hang out with people who make us feel natural and easy. And sometimes we don't talk at all; we just simply enjoy the warmth and comfort of another soul nearby.

But here on the Earth, people who Network and Build Relationships get something called Success, a condition greatly admired, that seems to have some connection with blonde hair, fit bodies, shiny cars, vast mansions and vacations on islands. But I could be wrong here. It's very confusing.

4. Earthlings Begin to Emerge in High School

Before high school, POPs often get along fairly well, especially since many of us have high intelligence in an abstract way, so that we are able to solve school problems easily. But high school has a set of strange rituals meant to sort out the Earthlings from the others. And these rituals only increase in College, where Success can often be predicted from the Relationships that are formed.

Earthlings seem to have an innate knowledge of how to act and dress for social success. They know how to fit in and exactly what to do during High School rituals. They get dates for the Prom, get elected to class office, wear Varsity Sweaters and go steady with each other. (I will not even try to explain what these things mean. They are completely foreign to interplanetary sensibilities.)

One real giveaway of an Earthling is that he or she LOVED school! For POPs, this time may have been very confusing and possibly deeply painful, causing long-lasting scars that seem to undermine our Success.

5. Earthlings Act in Their Own Best Interest

This characteristic is highly tied to their understanding of Cause and Effect and Delayed Gratification, as well as Relationship Building. Earthlings have a natural understanding of what will bring them Success in all areas of life and they actually take action that moves them closer to what they want, rather than farther away.

When they have a choice of action, they will do what works best for them. They seem to have real clarity about what they want, where they are going and how to get there. They are focused and clear and would not dream of doing something that would undermine their overall progress toward the fulfillment of their desires.

Some of them even have things they call Goals which have specific Tasks assigned, so that when you complete all of the Tasks on time, you achieve the Goal when you want to. Now that's Success!

I know, I know. I'm asking you to take in a lot of difficult concepts, but please do try to continue, because this is one of the most dangerous of the Earthling characteristics.

You see, on my planet we are all highly sensitive to other people's energies. And for this reason, our social rituals are built around being very considerate and not imposing our energies on another.

We POPs know how important this is, because we are so susceptible, so heavily influenced by others when they ramp up their energy. In fact, some POPs find themselves completely losing their center when they are with a strongly-projecting Earthling. They can't seem to help themselves. They buy things they don't want or need, they accept fantasy projections as real, they eat what is unhealthy for them, they even give away that which they hold dear.

When you are with people from your own planet, all the energies are soft and easy to be around. You can relax and know that they would never try to get you to do something you shouldn't or wouldn't do in order to promote their Success. They simply are and they allow you to be. You have no need to protect yourself, because you know that they are watching out for you and themselves both.

Earthlings can also be like this, when they are relaxed and not going after something they want. But POPs find it difficult to tell when Earthlings are being relaxed and generous and when they are Acting in Their Own Best Interests, Building Business Relationships and going after Success.

It is for this reason that a large part of the Earth Survival Guide is dedicated to discerning and dealing with Earthling Energies. Learning how to do this is vital for your health and your survival.

6. Earthlings are Comfortable in Their Bodies

Your basic Earthling seems to be very comfortable in this physical form, as difficult as this may be to understand. They enjoy movement and exercise and staying fit. They have great balance and are light on their feet, even in this extremely dense gravity. They are rarely clumsy and awkward, tripping and dropping things.

Here's a really easy way to identify an Earthling:

> *Question:* "When do you eat?"
> *Earthling Answer:* "When I'm hungry."

They eat when they're hungry. You really have to laugh.

Most any POP can tell you that food is a powerful drug, used to regulate and calm the uncomfortable emotions that seem to come along with the human form, such as unhappiness, happiness, anger, frustration, satisfaction, loneliness, anxiety, fun, sadness, despair, depression, boredom and shame, to name just a few legitimate reasons to eat. Chocolate is one of the better-known food drugs, but please don't discount donuts, cookies and pizza as excellent sources of refined carbohydrates, salt and fat, all of which are powerful antidotes to unwanted Earth Feelings.

There is a lovely side-benefit to eating a lot of flour, sugar, salt and fat. Not only does it taste quite good, but your own body soon accumulates a wall of fat that then cushions you from the painful earth energies. We POPs who pick up the emotions of everyone around us often feel a need to build that protective barrier.

There is a certain numbness that comes along with being really fat that can be quite comforting. I've also noticed fewer invitations to those noisy parties.

Of course, this is not the only POP defense against cruel Earth energy. Some POPs have made the opposite choice, which is to eliminate this troublesome body altogether by barely eating anything at all.

Both of these choices can lead to an early departure from the Earth, which has a lot going for it. The only problem is that you will probably get sick first, and then you're in the hands of Modern Medicine, which is not a place any of us want to go.

If you decide to try to be Comfortable in Your Body, please do not Diet. This is a painful ritual in which POPs periodically starve themselves in a desperate attempt to look like an Earthling only to regain all the weight and more.

Young, slender and incredibly fit Earthlings will tell you that all you have to do is Permanently Change Your Eating Habits in order to look like them. Good luck with that.

3
How We Got Here

I have heard some theories about how the Earth was seeded from other planets, and that we are the descendants of those early interplanetary settlers.

This may well be true, but it still does not explain the phenomena I see. Because if I were descended through those bloodlines, then that would mean that my grandparents, parents, siblings and cousins would all be from the same planet as I am. I think most of us would agree that this is clearly not the case, and that your family is made up of many vastly different species.

So here's my theory.

When a child is conceived, the quickening Soul Spirit has an opportunity to select a planetary bloodline as well as a collection of natural talents for this emerging being to explore and expand upon in their brief life here on Earth.

At that moment of conception, the Soul Spirit also draws a path of destiny in the sand. Knowing that the sand might be blown about before the path is seen, the Soul Spirit takes pity and places milestones here and there, marking the major events that pull us forward on the path we are here to walk.

For most of us, the winds blow early and hard, and we spend our lives wandering across the sand, drawn by those milestones without even knowing that they are there, until suddenly one of them flashes clean and clear before us.

But our Soul Spirit is always right there giving us guidance, if only we will pay attention to the clues given us: intuitive flashes of knowing, visions and inner voices, feelings in our heart and center and, of course, coincidence, serendipity and the whisper of angels.

In some cases, a child born on earth might be born an Earthling, in which case they can just use their innate Earthling skills that work so well here, and they may solve the puzzle of earth life without looking for clues.

But in my case, and quite possibly in yours, the bloodline came from some other distant planet in a far-off galaxy where things are quite different indeed, and these obscure clues are often of vast importance in finding your way.

HOW WE GOT HERE

It is my hope that the Earth Survival Guide will assist you. Here is a glossary of some of the most confusing Earth concepts to help you along your way.

4
Glossary of Some Earth Terms and Concepts

Below is a collection of Earth terms and concepts that are particularly confusing to POPs. To be fair to Earthlings, not all of this is caused by them. Much of it may be from the chaotic mix of interplanetary species we find here.

Regardless, as you read, please just know that you are not alone in feeling that this world makes no sense at all.

Religion: This is a group of people who share a common belief about how to live in loving and wise ways as well as a belief about what happens after we die. There are a lot of rules, ceremonies and traditions that have been around for thousands of years and are very important to Religious people.

Oddly, they may kill each other, even wage wars, because they don't like other Religions, all of which is deeply confusing to POPs.

Fundamentalists:
Fundamentalists believe absolutely in the literal truth of Religious documents written thousands of years ago. If you read the entire texts as they have come down to us, you would find them riddled with contradictions, but that appears not to be a concern.

Interestingly, Fundamentalists from all religions appear to agree on one thing: the importance of man's power over women on Earth. Again, this concept is confusing to most POPs, upon whose planets women are revered as the creators of life.

Do I think that Fundamentalists have the right to their deep beliefs? Of course! Do I wish they would keep them to themselves? Yes, please.

God:
Some Religions have explained the unexplainable by assigning responsibility to God, who is usually portrayed as an old white man in the clouds. This God is all-powerful, but quite capricious, punishing some people for rules that others are obviously allowed to break, killing some and saving others for no apparent reason. It's really quite nerve-wracking!

GLOSSARY OF SOME EARTH TERMS

And even though God has the power to intervene in life and death at will, the deepest believers in this power can't seem to wait to let God handle it, but feel it is up to them to punish the wicked and speed them off to the afterlife they so richly deserve.

No wonder both football teams get on their knees and pray before each game. If the other team prays and you don't, will you lose? But if both teams pray, what will God do then?   No one knows. Perhaps that's why the most devoted fans paint their faces purple or wear cheese hats; they are simply trying to please a very confusing God.

In an interesting twist, the Christians believe in the same God as the Jews, as evidenced by their Holy Bible, which tells the story of the Jews as God's favorites. And yet, Christians spent many a year persecuting Jews, until they finally felt so guilty they pretended no one was currently using Palestine and gave it to the Jews for their Country. Rather like the Europeans and North America: Oh, are there people living here?

As you can see, this God has a lot to answer for. Lately, however, an abbreviated God is sometimes used to indicate great surprise, delight and amazement, as in "OMG!!!! He's so cute!!"   This seems like a hopeful, upbeat trend, don't you think?

Those who are Spiritual, rather than Religious, may also use the word God, but mean by it a pervasive sense of Oneness or Spirit shared by all, a belief probably similar to that on your planet.

Coming full circle, many American Spiritualists now revere the practices of the Native Americans their ancestors wiped out. One can hardly blame the surviving Native Americans for thinking it's a bit late.

Evolution: Earth Science says that Earth organisms respond to the environment through the generations in an adaptive process called Evolution. According to the Survival of the Fittest, if the strongest and brightest breed more, then the species will eventually evolve into magnificence.

Certain Fundamentalist Religions disagree with Evolution, because they think it somehow challenges their belief that God created humans, apes and dinosaurs during the same week. One might, of course, simply understand this as a monumental failure to grasp the use of metaphor.

Some religions have required for centuries that their most educated and devout be celibate for life, which, if evolution is true, would inevitably result in a gradual decline in the power of that Religion.

Oops.

In another interesting twist, since Birth Control has been available, the most educated and successful Earthlings now have the least number of children. This may just be the opportunity for POPs to move in and up!

Jesus: Jesus was a Jewish day laborer who lived for only 30 years before he was killed by the Romans occupying his country. Despite this brief existence, of which we have no contemporaneous written record, his influence has been enormous. The Romans fed his followers to the lions for a few hundred years, then did an about-face, redid the entire calendar to begin on the day of his birth, and immediately began naming popes and killing people.

Jesus spoke of love and forgiveness, yet bloody wars have been fought in his name. Christians call him the Son of the Jewish God they worship, but the Jews deny this. Some paint his name in glitter on their vans and give odd rambling speeches about how he is going to come again and then we'll all be sorry.

Some think Jesus was a Christian, not a Jew. (Just think about that for a minute...)

Some think using his name will help a boy become a very good baseball player, which is apparently true.

Some POPs call him Yeshua, hoping to dissociate him from all this craziness. I understand this, because I have experienced Yeshua's energy directly, personally, and it is most beautiful, full of love, compassion and forgiveness, gentle yet quite intense. In fact, it may just be the loveliest energy I have experienced on Earth. No wonder everyone has made such a fuss about it.

Spirituality: This is for people who agree about living in loving and wise ways, but prefer not to follow the rules of Religion. They usually adopt only the portion of a belief or practice that corresponds with their own personal views, rather like choosing from a Chinese menu: I'll take Meditation from Column A, Shamanic Drumming from Column B, Reiki from Column C, and Yeshua for dessert.

Religious people, on the other hand, order from fixed price menus, all or nothing. They don't feel it is right to pick and choose. "Love it or leave it!" I may be a little confused here, though. I'm not sure if that statement refers to Religion or America. Oh well.

There used to be very few Earthlings who cared about Spirituality, but now it is Going Mainstream, which is beginning to confuse the POPs, who used to find it a safe haven.

GLOSSARY OF SOME EARTH TERMS

Going Mainstream: This is where ideas and practices, such as yoga, meditation and alternative medicine, that were once seen as weird and worthy of derision, are embraced by the Earthlings. When this happens, the practice usually becomes profitable, which attracts even more Earthlings, but for different reasons. Going Mainstream is usually seen as a good thing at the beginning, since the POPs actually get to make some Money doing what they do, but in the end, they may fall victim to the Earthlings who are Acting in Their Own Best Interests.

Money: This started as precious metal, then became pieces of paper, and now it is numbers within a computer, hurtling through space or sitting in a cloud. This abstract concept is used to determine whether someone eats truffles in a mansion on a hill or starves in a crowded slum.

A word to POPs: This is so important here on Earth, but good luck understanding it!

Truffles: People use pigs to locate this edible fungus in the forests of Europe and then sell it at an enormously high price, thus signifying that they have both Money and Good Taste.

No, I don't get it either.

Good Taste: This is a strong indicator of Earthlings, for it signals that they may have come from a long line of Earthlings, which can be very powerful indeed. Or they are very clever nouveau Earthlings who simply have a natural understanding of what is both In Good Taste from the past and what is *au courant* today, a subtle balance that only Earthlings truly understand.

Profit, Investment, Stocks, Markets, Economy, Margin, IBIT and so on: These are ways that Earthlings get more Money to buy more Truffles. You can live on Earth without knowing any of this, but do be careful and remember that these are the primary tools of the Earthling who is Acting in His Own Best Interests. You can accidentally get hurt by events they call Recession and Depression, and If you become an obstacle in the way, watch out!

Pollution, Global Warming, Air Quality Index, Pesticides, and so much more: There are few things as baffling as the way Earthlings have chosen to destroy the very planet that sustains them. Any well-traveled POP can tell you that Earth was once one of the most beautiful planets in the universe:

pristine waters, brilliantly fresh air, deep oceans and dense forests just teeming with amazing life forms.

Now the air quality index says whether it's safe for children to go outside to play and tampons wash up on the beaches. Asthma, autism and mysterious 'syndromes' are greatly on the rise and over 90% of Americans test positively for insecticides in their bodies.

OK, here's a good one for you. What's the difference between an Earthling and a light bulb? A light bulb doesn't screw itself.

Businesses and Corporations: These are more ways that Earthlings get money for Truffles, but they are also the mechanisms that most POPs must utilize, too, to put food on the table and a roof overhead. Oh, it's so indirect here on Earth!

But there's a big difference in how these tools are used: the Earthlings become CEOs and Successful Entrepreneurs in private jets and the POPs usually have a Day Job.

Advertising, Marketing and Sales: These are ways to get Money by letting people know how unattractive, inadequate and generally lacking they are and showing how your product will make them rich, sexy, desirable, healthy, happy and wise.

One of the best ways to make a lot of Money is to tell people you can teach them how to make Money, because then they are not just spending money for your advice or service, they are Investing in their Future.

Win/Win: This is where one who is Acting in His Own Best Interests teams up with others doing the same, thus forming a Team that works together for the benefit of all involved. This is seen as the ultimate Success, where one is allowed to demonstrate a superior nature while still caring for oneself.

This can be a way for Earthlings and POPs to work together as long as the POPs remember that it is up to them to watch their own interests and make sure their half of the Win doesn't turn into a Lose.

Mentoring: This is a strange Earth Business practice where you try to get someone you barely know to devote their time and energy into helping you to understand and follow Earth guidelines so that you will have Success.

Giving Back: This is where a CEO:
- Generates billions for his corporation by laying off thousands of workers in the United States and moving industry overseas

- Pollutes the overseas rivers with factory waste
- Retires with hundreds of millions in stock options
- Avoids taxes by creating a foundation to help people overseas get clean water by digging wells.

Is that harsh? You're right. To be fair, there are many perfectly lovely Earthlings, who use this term to mean that they were very fortunate in life and now they want to share their knowledge and prosperity with others less fortunate.

On my planet, there is no money or poverty, everyone has what they need and no one is more or less fortunate in this regard. Charity on Earth often seems odd to a POP, since it has an air of superiority about it. People who are Giving Back seem always to have first achieved Success by Acting in Their Own Best Interests. It's not wrong, mind you, and it's most often meant well, but it just gives one pause.

Trophy Wife: When a very successful male Earthling reaches Middle Age, he may trade in the mother of his children for a new model, usually slightly younger than his daughter, with blond hair, boyish hips, long legs and large breasts supplied by Modern Medicine.

He takes pills with alien-sounding names to keep her happy. Before marriage, she must sign a Pre-Nup, so that the Tennis Pro, who doesn't need Viagra or Cialus, stays On the QT.

The First Wife, meanwhile, enters a phase called Starting Over. First Wives may mate again, but they're usually a bit too savvy to remarry. They may become Ladies Who Lunch. They may Give Back. Or, if they were not the First Wife, but merely an Ex-Wife who signed a Pre-Nup, they get a Day Job.

Am I being too harsh? I mean no ill will. I hope that the young, new wife keeps her husband happy and healthy until he finally dies from exhaustion. But if she does end up care-giving for her husband and parents at the same time, I hope that she takes up with that Tennis Pro with no guilt pangs at all.

As for the ex-wife, I wish for her that she may enter the glory years of her life with head held high, finally having the freedom to focus on herself and grow into the Goddess that she truly is!

Feminism: Back in the '60s in the US, some women demanded equal rights with men. They called it Women's Lib and held consciousness-raising sessions, where they discussed how men were capable of learning to make the bed.

GLOSSARY OF SOME EARTH TERMS

Miss Jones, the Actress, became Ms. Jones, the Actor, yet she still wears her dresses cut down to here and her skirts up to there, and teeters on impossibly high heels. And she still earns a lot less Money and has a lot less Power than Mr. Jones who, incidentally, still doesn't make the bed.

All of this will seem a bit odd to POPs, who come from planets where women don't think twice about equality. They are, after all, 50% of the population most everywhere.

I don't begin to have the answers here, but I am toying with the idea that all this has something to do with Earth society's marginalization of those things that are natural to women. Women are natural intuitives who have been taught that psychic abilities are not real. They are natural healers who have been taught that only Modern Medicine and Science can heal. They blossom when they are in a cooperative community, yet must fit into hierarchical structures to get Money and Power. Many have a natural sensitivity and empathy that is their strength, yet they are taught that it makes them weak.

Women on Earth also seem especially vulnerable to a highly contagious Disease called Low Self-Esteem, which strips away their confidence and renders them full of self-doubt and unable to Act in their Own Best Interests. Could this be caused by high heels that make it hard to keep up, much less take the lead? I can't really say.

Many of these suffering women are simply POPs, who are living in the deep state of confusion that affects all POPs on earth. But I believe there is an opportunity here for all women, both Earthling and POPs, to unite and make things right on the Earth. After all, women's natural gifts are exactly what is needed here right now.

Well, not all Earthling women would be a part of this, of course. The ones who like to go out with their men and shoot Bambi can just stay home and make the bed.

Bitch: A derogatory term that refers to a woman who is behaving the way a man does when he is Acting in His Own Best Interests.

I almost took this entry out, just because I dislike this word sooo much! But it does need to be pointed out that this is what it really means, because it isn't widely recognized. After all, on my planet, women are admired for being strong, physically, mentally and emotionally. Of course they watch out for themselves and their children, just like any Lioness!

Day Job: This is what people do every day to earn enough Money to survive in Earth society. Some have what are called White Collar jobs, which means they work very long hours in windowless cubicles under fluorescent lights to put the children they rarely see through College, so that their children can then sit in cubicles for most of their day to pay off their College Loans.

People with Blue Collar Day Jobs often put in long hours in difficult environments, doing the necessary functions that keep society running smoothly, like cleaning the streets. Oddly, people who do these vitally important jobs have low Status and very little Money. Some need multiple Day Jobs at Minimum Wage to feed their families, and yet they continue having more and more children. It is a puzzling thing, that those who can least afford to support children often have the most. I will update the Survival Guide if I come to understand this better.

There used to be Blue Collar jobs in the United States in which people made things, belonged to Unions and were paid Money. These are now largely replaced by Minimum Wage Service Jobs, where the Day Job people serve each other Fast Food.

CEO: Someone who sits in a large corner office with windows, receives a very large Compensation Package that rewards increasing Profits and keeping up the Stock Price. The CEO often receives a large Bonus for eliminating Day Jobs and fighting to keep Minimum Wage as low as possible.

The CEO may not have a PhD, MD, MBA or CPA, but is usually quite proud of having Street Smarts and graduating from the School of Hard Knocks.

CEO's prefer Truffles to Fast Food, but may run large Fast Food companies, from which they earn the millions of dollars it takes to buy and keep a Trophy Wife.

Senior Citizens: On other planets, those who are old and wise are often revered and given places of honor in the family. This is true on Earth if they eat Truffles and have private jets. Then the daughters and Trophy Wives trade clothes during vacations in the Bahamas. "OMG, I *love* you in my pink polka dot bikini! Look, Daddy, doesn't she look great?"

But when Day Jobbers who don't understand Money get old, they gather in places called Senior Citizen Centers and play Bingo for dog food and cereal. But it's not all bad. Sometimes a granddaughter comes by with her piano teacher and puts on a terrific show.

And sometimes they actually give the dog food to a dog.

GLOSSARY OF SOME EARTH TERMS

Modern Medicine: This is where people use sharp instruments to cut into other people, sometimes to save a life and sometimes to try to make them look younger. In more recent years, it is also a dispensary of things called Pharmaceuticals or Drugs, which may save lives, but may also have so-called Side Effects, such as death, suicide and addiction.

Medicine is one of those areas, like Science, where the latest theory or practice is proclaimed as absolute Truth, but the Truth shifts and changes with time, like desert sands.

Cautionary Note to POPs, especially Senior Citizens: Be sure to sign something that allows you to die when your time comes. Oddly, it's called a Living Will. If you don't have one, Modern Medicine may keep your physical body breathing artificially, long after your spirit has departed. Actually, now that I think about it, I'm not sure this really matters. If they want this body, they can have it.

Both Earthlings and POPs appear to practice Medicine, but Alternative Medicine, which tries to avoid both sharp instruments and Drugs in favor of natural substances and practices, is more heavily populated by POPs. This is changing, however, as Alternative Medicine is now profitable and Going Mainstream.

Disease: If an unfortunate condition is officially named a Disease, then Modern Medicine can treat it and get reimbursed by Health Insurance. Sometimes a Disease may actually be created so that a new Pharmaceutical has something to cure.

The current trend is to call a Disease by its initials, thus giving it a bit of flair and panache. No longer does the embarrassed would-be lover shrink away in shame. Now he can say: "I'm being treated for ED, you know—you just need to be more patient and considerate!" We can all agree that is much better.

Placebo: This is a sugar pill used in a scientific double-blind trial to demonstrate that a new Pharmaceutical is more effective than nothing in treating a Disease. If the Pharmaceutical does not pass the trial, it will not be approved for sale, so there is a lot of Money at Stake, always a dangerous condition.

Unfortunately for Pharma companies, there is something called the Placebo Effect, where people who are given a sugar pill actually cure themselves of their Disease without needing the Pharmaceutical at all. The Pharma companies have pooh-poohed this effect quite convincingly and worked hard to keep these crazy people out of the trials.

As a POP, you will easily recognize the Placebo effect. On your planet, they called it Healing Yourself.

GLOSSARY OF SOME EARTH TERMS

On earth, people are taught that they cannot heal themselves, all evidence to the contrary. Because of this widespread belief in the impossibility of self-healing, they sometimes need to trick their minds with a Placebo to allow their bodies to work naturally.

Sports and Teamwork: Earthlings are very involved in Sports and absolutely revere Teamwork. In Sports, people try to show other people that they are superior to them by getting a ball and possibly their body to a designated place in a very particular way, with a lot of rules and restrictions and score-tallying. When they succeed, the people watching them, often wearing quite odd clothing that designates their team, cheer and sometimes even riot, proclaiming their superiority through projection with the victors on the field.

All of this is learned at a very young age and is said to build character and prepare one for the world of business. One of the more interesting early rituals is that after screaming and humiliating their children to spur them on to victory, the parents then ask them to perform a mock celebration of the other team, usually with a ritualized chant such as "2, 4, 6, 8, who do we appreciate?" This is said to demonstrate being a Good Sport, but appears to be teaching them not to show

how they really feel. Which is, of course, excellent preparation for business.

People who go on to become professional athletes and win a lot are highly compensated by Money and Status, including the ability to mate with a superior Earthling, quite possibly young and blonde.

Elephants and Donkeys: These are the Political Parties in the government of the United States, sometimes called Republicans and Democrats, respectively. The Elephants appear to be most supportive of CEOs and the Donkeys more supportive of "common" people, but one suspects that the leaders of both parties are simply Earthlings Acting in Their Own Best Interests.

Both parties seem to enjoy a periodic ritual where they wear funny red, white and blue hats, carry placards with people's names and yell a lot, much like the fans at Sports venues. Then they choose champions to fight a battle against the other party.

Elephants and Donkeys are not nearly as highly compensated in Money as Sports Idols, even when they win, but they may have even more Status as well as the power to get Truffles in other ways. They may also get to keep their jobs longer, even into senility, whereas the Sports Idols have very short careers. Also, male politicians don't need to be as good-looking as male Sports Idols.

Female politicians are required to wear makeup, have facelifts and do everything they can to look young and attractive. All female politicians know that it is dangerous to be too outspoken, authoritative and intelligent, but they also need to be careful not to go too far the other direction. It is indeed a thin line to walk, which may be why they wear lower heels.

Patriots: The earth is divided into various areas called Countries. Patriots are the people who associate deeply with some Idea that the Country stands for, whether or not the actions of that Country actually reflect that Idea.

Some of these Ideas are fairly harmless, like wearing Lederhosen and playing the accordion at weddings. But some Ideas are very dangerous, amounting to a License to Kill. The Patriots with a License to Kill wear clothing that conveys Power, not silly Lederhosen.

Some countries have lots of rules to keep other people out. Some have rules to keep people in. Some mark their boundaries by rivers and mountains, some by barbed wire. Some countries fight to take over other countries, though all they really gain is something called Power. Oh, yes, and Money for their

Leaders, for a Country does not need to earn Money, it can just Tax people.

Oddly, Earthlings do not seem to notice that a Country is not a real thing. People kill and die, some people get very rich and others lose everything, the wars begin and end, the barbed wire goes up and down, then different people get rich and different ones lose everything, all to no apparent purpose.

A note of caution to POPs: It is this blindness of the Patriot that is particularly dangerous. Like Religion, Patriotism is learned very, very young and does not easily bend or change. Be very careful and always consider a Patriot to be armed and dangerous.

America: This refers to the most influential Country in the continent of the Americas. More than that, though, America is an Idea that many Patriots believe in fervently, even though there is overwhelming evidence that the Idea isn't quite working.

The American Idea is that there is equal opportunity, even though 90% of the Money is held by 10% of the people. The American Idea is written on the Statue of Liberty ("Give me your tired, your poor..."), even though America is building a wall to keep out immigrants. The American Idea is freedom and free expression, even though America spies and eavesdrops on everyone, including Americans. The American Idea is continual growth and expansion, even though the CEOs, Elephants and Donkeys have given away what was once an extravagant opportunity for a strong and growing middle class in exchange for Truffles for the few. The American Idea is that Americans are good, caring people, even though America puts drones in the sky to silently kill people as they walk down the street to the store.

Still, the American Ideas are great. And Thomas Jefferson certainly had a way with words, even if he did have sex with his slaves. But the Ideas, the Ideas are great.

Truth: On the Earth, Truth is much more situational than it is on my planet. On my planet, there is a Truth that lives within and it does not change. People who are Truthful are those who speak from that place. You can recognize their Truth by its wise and loving nature and the way it lifts everyone and everything.

On the Earth, Truth may change from moment to moment and person to person. Sometimes it seems to be simply a tool for Patriots and other Earthlings who are Acting in Their Own Best Interests.

Cautionary note to POPs: the more someone professes how honest he is, the less honest he is likely to be.

I know, I know. It's hard to know how to survive in a place where truth cannot be trusted. But that's just the way it is here.

Sex: It is very easy for POP's to understand what Sex is, since all the planets have some way for a species to reproduce, but it is extremely confusing to grasp the Earthling views on it. If you can understand Sex and Money, you will have come a long way toward surviving on Earth.

Earth sex feels really good and I highly recommend it. Most everyone, POPs and Earthlings alike, agree that Sex is pleasurable, but some people only enjoy it if they inflict or receive pain. I don't think these are Earthlings, though. I think they may be from a very dark planet, though it's hard to say. I know they are not from my planet, where we enjoy laughing a lot during sex.

Some Earthlings, especially Religious ones, believe it is sinful to enjoy sex, which may lead to a condition called Guilt. This is because they go ahead and have sex anyway, because it feels so good.

There is a very interesting phenomenon, where the people who most preach the evils of sex, and often earn a good deal of Money in doing so, are found to be secretly engaged in sexual acts, frequently and with many people. This used to be called a Scandal. It is now called Sexual Addiction, which means they really weren't having any fun, so it wasn't a sin and they don't need to feel Guilt. It also means they can be cured of the Disease by Modern Medicine or a 12-Step Program.

Note to POPs: I know, on your planet you could probably just walk up to someone attractive and suggest having Sex. Do not do that on Earth. You could lose your Day Job. And even outside of work, there is a complicated ritual of conversation and drinking alcohol that seems to be required to Get to First Base.

12 Steps and 10 Commandments: These are frequently referred to as being deeply important, but interestingly, no one can actually name them.

Note to POP's: It is OK to laugh and have fun while trying to come up with the names of the 7 Dwarves or the 8 Reindeer. You can even mock-fight about whether Rudolph makes it 9. But you may deeply offend someone by making fun of the 12 Steps, especially people who wear necklaces with numbers and talk about their friend Bill.

And never, ever, take the 10 Commandments lightly. Your life could depend upon it.

Sexual Identity and Orientation: This is too confusing to even try to explain. It is not as simple as what body parts you have and what your role is in making babies. It's not even as simple as how and with whom you enjoy having Sex.

For example, there are some men who have their bodies changed by Medicine to almost look like women. They then earn the right to wear scarves, nail polish and lipstick without being considered Gay. If they have sex with women, are they Lesbians? No one knows. And nowadays, fewer and fewer people even care.

There are some natural-born women who aren't interested in scarves and lipstick at all. Of course, an aggressive woman without lipstick could be accused of being a secret Lesbian, even though she doesn't have sex with other women. This may be why very aggressive women often wear a lot of makeup.

Some men are very ashamed that they enjoy wearing women's clothing, especially lacy underwear, so they do it secretly at night, alone. But women are allowed to wear men's clothing openly. There was even a time, called the Eighties, when women wore exaggerated shoulder pads, as part of Fashion, which is a whole study in itself. The masculine shoulder pads were offset by Big Hair, however, making the whole effect, well, beyond description.

GLOSSARY OF SOME EARTH TERMS

Everyone here on earth is so confused about sex, that it is really impossible to tell which things are Earthling characteristics and which things are brought here from other planets. I suspect that those who are not comfortable with their sexual identity on Earth are POPs and that when they chose their planetary bloodline and gender during conception, the characteristics of the galactic gender just didn't quite mesh with the Earth body.

But I could be completely wrong about this.

Love: On your planet you probably have many words for the many different ways to love: love of a friend, love combined with sexual yearning, mature love of a lifetime partner, love of a child, love of work, love of family, love of God or Spirit, to name just a few. You also have different words that convey the intensity of the love, ranging from "I love you so much I don't know how I could ever live without you" to "Oh, I just love this blue sweater!" You probably have nuances in the language that convey the likely duration of the feeling, from "I'll always love you" to "I love you, but I'm going away to college next year."

On Earth, there is one word that covers all of this. This amazing lingual inadequacy causes confusion. It also conveys the underlying problem in Earth society, which is that something so deeply and fundamentally important for a fulfilling life is treated to so little attention.

And yes, the same problems exist with the word Hate.

Right-to-Lifer: This is a person who believes that the rights of the unborn fetus are more important than the rights of those already born, especially pregnant women. Some Right-to-Lifers believe this so strongly, that they are willing to kill those who do not agree, so do be careful.

Interestingly, the same people who profess the Sanctity of Life often support Capital Punishment, which is the state's right to kill those who break rules. But after all, Capital Punishment is never inflicted upon the unborn fetus, so there is a kind of consistency to it.

There is something called Abortion that people are very passionately for and against. On my planet, women are so completely in tune with their bodies that they know whether having sex would result in pregnancy. If they want to have sex during their fertile time, they simply ask a man they would like to have as the father of their children. A man would never dream of forcing a woman to have sex against her will. And since there is no money and everyone has everything they need, no one would find a child a burden. Hence, this is not an issue. But here on earth, none of that is true.

For the last 50 years or so, there has been something called Birth Control that has made Abortion less necessary. Interestingly, many of the same people who are against Abortion are also against Birth Control. This apparent conflict seems to have something to do with a Religious belief in the evils of pleasurable Sex Outside of Marriage. But those same people are usually against Gay and Lesbian Sex as well, which doesn't require Birth Control or lead to Abortion. And they are particularly opposed to Gay Marriage.

Yes, you're right, it's beyond understanding. Don't even try.

School: This is an institution of learning. Unlike learning on most planets, on Earth you spend most of your time learning to correct what you do poorly, like teaching cats to swim. Very little time is spent in discovering natural, unique talents and lifting them into genius.

Training is begun early by setting a lot of behavioral rules and ringing bells to let children know when it is time to work, talk and walk. In college, those who go on to eat Truffles will major in Bell Ringing, also known as Delegating.

Many POPs learn the subtle art of fitting in and getting by, while secretly developing their own unique talents and powers. These talents are usually dismissed by Earthlings as Unprofitable, but some lucky POPs find someone to encourage and help them, usually an older POP.

Every so often a POP becomes a Rock Star by being in the right place at the right time and catching a ride on a rising trend. When this happens, they become A-List Celebrities and earn lots of Money. They are invited to parties where Earthlings give them lots of free merchandise, which would have been helpful when they were struggling, but which now they could easily just buy.

These are dangerous times indeed for the unsuspecting POP. Be very careful of Win-Win Deals offered by Earthlings Acting in Their Own Best Interests or you may quickly find yourself Last Year's News.

Supernatural, Paranormal, Extra Sensory Perception (ESP), Psychic and Mind Reading:
All of these terms describe the natural intuitive senses that all humans possess. For some reason, modern society, especially in the West, has chosen to teach that these senses are not real. It's hard

to believe, I know, but at one time, women were actually burned at the stake for using these natural skills. Even now, the use of these senses is still sometimes seen as some sort of dark art performed by weird misfits.

Many Earth people actually do know that they have these skills and they use them all the time, they just pretend they don't. Schools teach that they are not real, but they are built into the language. Women's Intuition, for example, which somehow manages to sound demeaning. And Gut Feeling, a wonderful phrase that allows a man to be intuitive and still manly.

Of course, on your planet, these same abilities were highly prized and led to great advances for civilization. It's just another of the Earth things that we will never quite understand.

Manifestation of Abundance:

This is a codified practice by POPs who are attempting to get Money and Relationships on the Earth by using what worked back home in their galaxy, *i.e.*, by simply projecting energy. It sometimes seems to work on Earth, but not predictably so, and not for everyone.

Face it, you just don't have the kind of power here on Earth that you're used to and the same things just don't always work.   Sometimes Earth just seems made of Kryptonite.

There are flows of energy blowing through the universe and across the Earth and sometimes what you desire just happens to be the same as what is flowing through, and you can catch a ride.

This can also happen to Earthlings. Normally, they think they caused it by Setting Goals and Acting in Their Own Best Interests. But if they happen to be doing regular Affirmations at the time that they catch the flow, they think they caused it through Positive Thinking and call it The Secret.

But there are times when what we desire in our hearts corresponds to the path drawn in the sand by Soul Spirit in that moment of conception. In these times, we may receive guidance and direction, take a deep breath and act with courage. Then things fall into place and the world unfolds to us in most magical and mystical ways.

Star Trek: This was an early television show that popularized some important POP concepts, such as allowing life forms to live as they wish. From this show, Earthlings learned the concept of the Vulcan Mind Meld as well as what to say when they feel the way we nearly always do and just want to get out of here: "Beam me up, Scottie!"

PART II

How to Survive (Even Thrive) On Earth

5

How to Survive (Even Thrive) on Earth

Did you sense a bit of frustration and dismay in what I wrote about Earth and Earthlings? Well, it might have just ended there, except for the most extraordinary thing that happened.

But before I go into my story, I need to tell you this: I talk to Spirit. Well, to be more precise, I listen to Spirit and then share what I receive. Right now, I share live sessions with Spirit on i-am-this.com in what I call Empowerments, a combination of spoken messages, visualizations and energy healings that help people transform into more magnificent versions of themselves.

By Spirit, I mean that voice of higher wisdom and truth. And I am pleased to include in my definition many forms of Spirit, just as long as they come from love. My personal experience has included, in no particular order: Jesus (aka Yeshua), God (aka an endless list of names), power animals, angels, archangels, goddesses, spiritual entities, faeries and intergalactic presences. Yours may include more or less than this, but in my definition, all forces of love, light, wisdom and truth are gladly welcomed.

If you are unconvinced that any of this exists, then try this exercise.

- Sit quietly and relax
- Close your eyes
- Pull back and watch yourself sitting and relaxing
- And now ask: Who is doing the watching?

You have just experienced yourself in two aspects. There is your physical self, that you were watching, and there is.... what?

Some call this presence the Watcher or the Witness. You might also say it is the soul or the higher self. But you know it, you feel it, as not the same as the physical body, yet it is you. It doesn't age or decay. And you may sense that it probably doesn't die, but rather is the eternal part of you. You may also sense that it is the source of truth, which loves and guides you.

Now, after you get a bit more familiar with the Witness, you may spread that energy out sideways, so that you begin to encompass all that surrounds you.

Let everything dissolve into particles of light. You may also lift yourself up higher so that you become one with the heavens, and lower, so that you become one with the earth. You may expand endlessly, until you know that you are one with everything else that exists. You are the universe and the universe is contained within you.

And then, if you choose, you may call this expanded presence God or Oneness or the Great All. Or the Field of Being. Or Spirit.

I have chosen to call it Spirit.

6
The Extraordinary Thing that Happened

One morning, after I finished receiving a message from Spirit, a different voice spoke in my head, a voice I recognized as The Ancient One. The Ancient One is a sperm whale as old as Earth herself, who lives in the deepest place in the ocean. I have encountered him before and have deep respect for his wisdom.

After a few moments, I realized that The Ancient One was dictating a story to me!

I raced to my computer, calling out: "Hold on, wait just a minute."

The voice stopped and politely waited.

"OK," I said, opening a new document on my computer . "Begin again, but more slowly this time."

The voice began again, moving at a slow and steady space, pausing whenever I asked it to pause, even for long rest breaks. Whenever I returned and asked it to begin again, it did.

And what it gave me was a story of Earth and the Planet Ur.

And now I am delighted to share it with you.

7
The Planet of Ur

Here is what I received:

Millions and millions of years ago, almost before time began, there was a planet named Ur. And what an amazing place it was, rich with plants and animals of all kinds, jungles and forests just teeming with life, rivers and oceans flowing with vibrant energy, the life force fairly bursting to be seen and known.

And when night fell on Ur, an enormous violet moon appeared and what a sight to behold it was. The air was filled with violet strands of light, purples and blues, streaks of pink here and there. And night-blooming orchids opened their faces to the moon and sang as they released their perfume to flow out like the streams of light across the land.

If you were able to go back in time to the glory years of Ur, and traveled all over this vast planet, you would be surprised to find that all of the animal forms you know from Earth, from all time, were there on Ur. On one continent the brontosaurus and tyrannosaurus roamed, magnificent beasts! On another you would find white wolves howling under the violet moon and oceans full of dolphins, sharks and manta rays. All animals now known to the earth were there on Ur. In fact, they were on Ur first.

And there were other animals on Ur as well, animals that have been dreamt of on Earth, but never seen, such as the glowing unicorn, the fire-breathing dragon and the flaming phoenix. Ah, yes, these were not mythical or imaginary. On Ur, they were very real indeed.

There were also men and women on Ur, who lived as the other animals did, just roaming the land and being alive, eating the berries of summer and storing up nuts in the caves for the winter.

And in the deepest ocean, at the very bottom, as deep as deep can be, was a sperm whale known as The Ancient One. The Ancient One was the first animal on Ur and he held all of the knowledge of what had ever happened there. No one knew of a time before The Ancient One, for no such time existed.

All life on Ur was aware of The Ancient One and he could be reached by just opening the mind. He held the wisdom of the land. When there were larger questions to be addressed, it was always The Ancient One who supplied the answers.

THE PLANET OF UR

And then, for no discernable reason, Ur began to die. The rivers dried up and the plants shriveled. Ice expanded here and deserts expanded there. The bounty began to fade and life became a struggle for survival.

Appeal after appeal flew through the mind space to The Ancient One. Help us! We are dying! Ur is dying! And so, The Ancient One formed a plan.

Out of his endlessly powerful mind, he created a Spirit Ark, a beautiful and bountiful place where the plants and animals could exist in spirit form, without needing a physical form, for that form could no longer be sustained on Ur. All creatures large and small transformed themselves into Spirit and found a home in the Spirit Ark, including The Ancient One himself.

And then, one day, when the physical planet Ur was barren, still and lifeless, The Ancient One launched the Spirit Ark in search of a new world.

How many light years passed in the journey? Thousands? Millions? How many miles were traveled? Millions upon millions? Only The Ancient One remembers.

Here I asked The Ancient One to stop for a while so I could rest—and absorb all of this. I wondered where this fascinating tale was leading us!

8
Earth and the Land of Ur

When I was ready to continue, I thanked The Ancient One for his patience. Then we moved forward with the story.

One day, The Ancient One saw the Earth shining in his mind's eye. He saw the beauty of this new emerging planet, with water flowing fresh from snowy mountains into oceans deep enough to hold The Ancient One himself. He saw the fertile soil and the pure blowing air and he knew, at last, here was home.

He brought the Spirit Ark to the Earth and deep, deep within the earth he found a place for it to reside, and he named it The Land of Ur.

Ah, what a joyous celebration it was, to be here at last on a planet so much like Ur once was. And yet, they were still Spirit, not physical. Which was very nice, of course, and very powerful, since as Spirit they had no limitations, but the joys of physical life were still remembered.

"The crunch of snow under my feet," Blacktoes Polar Bear said, "I miss that."

"And leaping out of the water and into the sky," said Finn Dolphin, "I miss that."

"Howling at the violet moon," said Brighteyes Wolf, "I miss that."

"Roaring out my beauty," said Braveheart Lion, "I miss that."

The Ancient One thought and thought. Finally he came up with another plan, an experiment, really, an adventure. Some animals would be allowed to take physical form on the earth. But their physical lifetime would be limited. They would be born onto the earth, grow up and live off the bounty of what they find on the land. After a time they would grow old and their physical body would die, returning to the soil, ashes to ashes, dust to dust. But after their time on the earth as a physical form, they would be able to return as Spirit to the Land of Ur.

For the first experiment, The Ancient One chose the animals that were the biggest and fiercest, the ones he believed would have the best chance of survival: the dinosaurs. They were so proud to be chosen! They exuberantly launched their life on earth, while the others remained in the Land of Ur and watched.

But there were several surprises. A delightful surprise was the discovery that once born upon the earth, they could actually reproduce there. So the original colony grew and thrived, for millions of years. Other animals joined the dinosaurs as well, leaping in the ocean, crawling on the land and flying in the skies.

There was another surprise that was deeply disturbing, however. Some of the animals felt their bodies shift and change. They developed an insatiable desire to eat other animals. No, it was more than a desire, it was an imperative, an all-consuming need to eat the flesh of other animals in order to live. And so they began to hunt and prowl.

And it was horrifying, of course, for The Ancient One to see this happening. But it was most horrifying for the little animals who suddenly found themselves on the menu for the larger animals, especially since they had all once been close friends.

The Ancient One tried to shift the energy, but he could not. He finally concluded that it must be a virus that existed on the Earth before they arrived, and it infected only some of the animals. Some were immune; some were only slightly infected and some were completely given over to this new appetite. He tried to call all the carnivores back to the Land of Ur, where he might be able to cure them of this dire illness. But they did not come.

And so it continued, generation after generation. Gradually, the animals on Earth adapted. Those who were smaller learned how to hide or protect themselves, at least some of them, some of the time. And those with the big teeth and great hungers killed only what they needed to survive. And a sort of balance settled upon the Earth, even though it was one that made The Ancient One deeply uncomfortable.

And then one day The Ancient One felt it coming. A giant comet was coming straight for earth. Oh, it was like the end of Ur all over again! A giant cloud covered the earth, blocking out the sun. Plants and animals died. Devastation was upon them.

Over time, the earth healed herself. Some species of animal had survived in physical form. Others, like the dinosaur, were no longer on the surface of earth at all. The Ancient One asked them if they wanted to return, but they were now happy just to remain in the Land of Ur. "Let some others go," they said. "Let some other species have a turn."

And so, gradually, this is what they did. As a species wanted to try out being physical on earth, they asked The Ancient One to give them form, which he did, but he never knew beforehand if they would catch the virus and turn out to be flesh-eaters.

Some species died out eventually and returned to exist only in the Land of Ur. Some never left the Land of Ur, like the unicorn, winged horse and dragon.

My mind was reeling. Carnivorous-ness was a virus. And so-called mythical beings were real in the Land of Ur. It was a lot to absorb.

9
Humans Join in the Fun

I refocused on the transmission. I didn't want to miss a word!

> *When humans decided to have an earth adventure, at first they were just as they had been on Ur, just another species of animal roaming the earth, being physical and alive. But as they reproduced, something strange happened to them.*
>
> *The human brain started developing in a very unique way, with a great increase in reasoning ability, allowing it to solve highly complex problems. But along with this ability came a highly critical view of things that began to see most everything as a problem to be solved. The brain not only regulated emotions and physical response to them, but also began to speak aloud in the mind in a most fearful way, seeing the world as a dangerous place and anything unfamiliar as deeply threatening. As this voice of fear spoke more and more loudly, the ancient fight-or-flight responses became increasingly*

prevalent, with hormones flooding through the body caused by remembered and imagined threats, not just the reality of a tiger in the jungle.

Humans became aggressive and territorial, killing each other and other species, not just for survival, but for power and control. They were driven by fear. Fear of someone else taking what was theirs, fear of not having enough, fear of not being enough, fear of losing out. These fears, and the doubts that came along with them, became the primary driver in society.

The Ancient One was deeply troubled. He tried, over and over, to call them back, to ask them to simply leave the earth and come back to the Land of Ur, so that they might be healed. Perhaps then they could go back to earth as the beautiful, clever animals they once were. But they were out of control and would no longer listen.

The Ancient One could see how miserable and unhappy they were. He could also see the future, where this rampant fear was not only harming the humans themselves, but was destroying Mother Earth. He could see that their fear-based greed would cause them to be more and more destructive as that brilliant human reasoning power was turned toward combating imagined fear.

HUMANS JOIN IN THE FUN

> *He saw images that no one should have to see, mushroom clouds of destruction rising into the sky.*
>
> *But he could not get them to stop. And he could not get them to return to the Land of Ur.*
>
> *Finally, he gathered the Ur animals together. He said, "Take pity on them, these humans. Forgive them. They have a mutation in the human brain that causes a voice to speak inside their heads, telling them that they are threatened, and must do these horrible, violent things. They think that voice speaks truth, but it is full of lies. It tells them that diamonds, gold and power are more important than love. It fills them with fear and tells them that they are alone and must protect themselves. It fills them with doubt and makes them think that all of the possibilities have already been used up."*

I had to pause here in receiving the transmission from The Ancient One. So this was it. The Earthling brain had mutated. I believed it. Even as a POP living inside an Earth human body, I could hear that voice inside the human brain lying to me, trying to make me afraid.

I hope The Ancient One is going to come up with some good solutions, I thought. Please, let there be some help for us here on this beautiful planet.

I asked The Ancient One to continue transmitting.

The animals had seen all of this and they agreed that the humans were indeed objects of great pity. But didn't they need to be stopped? Couldn't that be done somehow?

The Ancient One said this: "There is only one way to save the earth now. And that is for enough humans to reach deep inside and find their truth and live from there. Truth still lives within each person, in the silence that lies between the thoughts. It still hangs in the air, in the beauty of a song. It still resides in the eye, in the glory of each setting sun. One person at a time, reaching within, knowing and living truth, will make the change. And once the humans stop destroying her, the earth will heal herself, as she always has."

The Ancient One continued. "We will do this. I will send out a call to the universe that People from Other Planets may come to help out. They will be known as POPs. When a baby is conceived on the earth, they will have a moment to choose their planetary heritage. Many will choose to be POPs. They will be born on the earth and live among the humans. They may even think they are humans for a time, but each will come to an awakening, when they realize that the earth society doesn't make sense and that they can begin to make a change, to make earth more like the wonderful planets from which they came. These POPs will begin to shift the energy among humans on the earth, until even the natural-born Earthlings see what is needed and begin to change."

Now I really had to pause and take a few deep breaths. That was exactly what had happened to me! I had awakened, I had discovered that I must be from another planet. And now here it was — I was right! But what a wonderful thing to learn that there is hope. I do hope they tell me how to begin that shift — I'm ready!

10
How Power Animals Came to Be

I asked The Ancient One to continue with this fascinating tale.

Pachy Elephant spoke next. "But what about us? We can't just stand by and watch this destruction without being able to do anything. Even my might is no longer a match on the physical earth for this human destruction. I need to do something from the Land of Ur."

The animals all nodded. They wanted to help. "There must be something we can do," they said. "Tell us how to help. Tell us what do to."

The Ancient One thought hard and long. Then he said this. "Those of you who wish to help the humans find truth, come with me." And he took them to a place with soft sand and a shining ocean. As the sun set, they gasped in amazement as the violet moon of Ur rose in the sky and the Ur orchids again sent their perfume across the land. Brighteyes Wolf began to howl with joy!

"Henceforth, you will be known as Power Animals, granted the power of the Violet Moon of Ur. If a human, Earthling or POP, asks you to join them, you will have the power to bring your wonderful characteristics to them, to strengthen them and to bring them closer to truth. Braveheart Lion's courage and confidence, Pachy Elephant's strength, leadership and power, Finn Dolphin's capacity for joy, all of this will be granted to them, when they ask.

"You will have the power to restore their body's ability to heal itself. You will have the power to stretch out those noisy thoughts so that they can find that little spot of silence that exists between the thoughts, the silence that is the entrance to peace and truth.

"You will have the power to fill their hearts with love so that they remember who they truly are and begin to create lives of joy and beauty. You will have the power to remind them that love is the answer and the only answer, that love and connection will heal their personal wounds, their society and then, slowly, the earth herself."

"But how will they know to ask us?" Red Fox cried out. "How will they even know we exist?"

"They have always known you exist," The Ancient One responded. "You have always been with them in their stories and hearts, even those of

HOW POWER ANIMALS CAME TO BE

you, like Mysty Unicorn, that never took physical form. Some people will find you on their own. But there will also be special POPs who will come forward to lead them to you. They may be known by such titles as Shaman, Medicine Man, Pathfinder or Wayfinder. They will appear."

Ah, yes, there it was. Of course. Shamans had been speaking out and helping societies for thousands of years. There had been some very dark times indeed, when they were named witches and rooted out from society, but now more and more were coming forward again. And I was one of them. I had been working with Power Animals. I had visited the Land of Ur and seen the Violet Moon. But I had been unable to draw enough attention to it.

But I had a feeling all of that was about to change. Perhaps with this *Earth Survival Guide*, it would be different, perhaps the time would now be right to spread the word and bring all this power to people.

I signaled for the transmission to continue.

"Will they come here or will we go there?" asked Ingrid Leopard, who was always very concerned about being some place with lots of spots.

"Both," replied The Ancient One. "I am granting you the power to exist in Spirit form on the earth. You will be able to take up residence in the heart and mind of a human who wishes to move into truth. They will ask a Shaman or Pathfinder to come retrieve you from the Land of Ur. And then you will be joined with them and help them navigate their way through earth society, to build a better, kinder, more compassionate and loving world, one based on truth."

"What if I don't want to go?" asked Legs Ostrich. "What if I don't even like them?"

The Ancient One nodded. "I understand," he said. "And I would never ask you to take up residence in the heart and mind of a human if you don't want to. Here's how it will work.

"If a human, Earthling or POP, has the foresight and wisdom to ask for your help, they will ask a shaman to come here for them. The shaman will enter the earth through a pool of water in a cave or sliding down the roots of a tree, will go down a tumbling passage and come out into The Land of Ur."

"After they reach the Land of Ur and start walking, what then?" asked Rory Mouse. Rory was very excited about this possibility. Finally something big and powerful to do, just like Braveheart Lion!

HOW POWER ANIMALS CAME TO BE

"When you see a shaman in the Land of Ur, you will have the power to know the human the shaman is representing. You will discern everything about her life on earth, the voice she has been listening to in her head, the yearning that lies within her heart. You will see and know all of it. And you will also know if you are the one who can bring her to truth. You will know this in your heart. And if you have this knowing, and if you are brave enough, you will come forward and show yourself to her in four aspects, perhaps front, back, right side and left side."

"And then the shaman has to accept us?" asked Rory Mouse, hoping the answer was yes.

"No indeed. But if you are accepted, you and the shaman will be transported back to the cave, where the human is waiting. The shaman will then perform a ceremony to blow your essence into her heart and head. And then you will dwell within her, sharing your energy, health, guidance and power."

I had studied how the shamans in various societies retrieved Power Animal spirits to heal people. And I had done quite a bit of this myself, acting as a pathfinder in private sessions and also by building a website, www.PowerAnimalsUnleashed.com, which provides an Enchanted Forest as the pathway to the Land of Ur.

I just hadn't known before how it had all started. How generous of the Power Animals to help us find our way!

"Then we are agreed?" The Ancient One asked. There was a chorus of approval from the Land of Ur. "And so it is," he declared.

And here the transmission stopped.

But that couldn't be it! They had developed this plan, they had offered themselves up as helpers, had invited POPs to come here as shamans and taught them how to retrieve power animals. All that had occurred.

But it hadn't been enough. The mushroom-cloud future The Ancient One had seen had come to pass. We were quickly destroying the Earth and continuing to kill each other. Now what?

Hadn't I received this for a reason? Wasn't there something else I was supposed to do? Surely, there must be.

I saved the file on my computer, but in deep confusion. Was this it?

11
Oscar Appears

The next day, my alarm went off amidst vivid dreams of the Land of Ur. When I first woke up, I thought the transmission from The Ancient One and the Land of Ur itself were all a dream. But gradually it felt like something remembered, something real. Had it happened? Had I really received messages and written it all down?

I rushed to my computer and saw the transcription I had done. Yes, it was true, it was actually true!

I conducted the daily Empowerment for the i-am-this.com members. It was a beautiful meditation about limitless possibilities.

After I hung up from the Empowerment, I took a deep breath, closed my eyes, went down into the silent Oneness and said: "Speak to me, Ancient One. Speak to me with your deep wisdom. I await your words."

After a minute, a voice spoke in my mind, but it was not The Ancient One.

"Hello, Carrie. It is I, Oscar."

My heart jumped. Could it be? Could this be my wonderful, perfect Oscar, the Orange Tabby who sat right next to my desk for 14 years, my dear, dear friend?

"Oscar! I have missed you so!"

"I am always with you. Always. I am in your heart and in your memory and now, I am in your mind speaking to you as well."

"How can that be, Oscar? How can I understand you?"

"The Ancient One has granted you the power to speak the language of Spirit. Soon you will begin to sing it in songs you are meant to share with those on earth. It speaks only truth and holds much power. You are deeply privileged to know it."

"Please convey my thanks to The Ancient One. And by the way, Oscar, why do you have a British accent?"

"Did you not sense my inherent dignity when I lived with you?"

OSCAR APPEARS

"I certainly did. Absolutely."

"This accent is merely to reinforce that. It's something you associate with the dignity that I am. And now, we must begin. We have much work to do."

"Do we? What are we doing?"

"As you heard, we have been trying to help humankind since the beginning. It worked reasonably well for thousands of years, by training the shaman, medicine man, witch and sorcerer how to access us and keep people in check. It was painful to watch their persecution and decline. But the last century, since the so-called industrial revolution, has been a complete disaster and now everything, including the planet, is in jeopardy."

"I certainly can't disagree. But what can we do?"

"There has been a meeting in the Land of Ur. The Ancient One has asked that we develop an up-to-date Earth Survival Guide for Earthlings and POPs. Since the decline in shaman power in

society, we believe it is necessary to teach Earthlings directly how to save themselves. And the expansion in global communication now allows us to do this."

"Count me in! There's just one thing. I'm concerned that humans don't understand their power to make this happen. They are trained to think that all power is from the outside. And I know this just isn't true.

"Earth always strives to renew. The daisy pushes through the crack in the sidewalk and reminds us that there is ever-surging life underneath, just waiting to express itself.

"I believe that it is still retrievable. I believe that the Earthlings and POPs that inhabit earth are capable of awakening to a new way. And I believe that when that happens, the energy on Earth will shift and we will find our way to wisdom.

"I believe this will come not through science and technology and not through the efforts of our minds, coming up with brilliant ideas and pushing them down upon people and the Earth.

"This will come one person at a time, from the inside out, as a new way of being is born in the heart and center. I believe that it will come as individual people awaken to their power and beauty, like a light coming on in the darkness. And as more and more lights come on, there will be a glow that becomes so strong that it shifts the energy on Earth and allows us to truly live from the heart and forge ways that are not apparent to the mind alone."

> *"We in the Land of Ur believe this as well. And that is why you and I are being asked to create an Earth Survival Guide to help accomplish this.*
>
> *"Why don't we start by having you tell the humans what you know about them, about each of them?"*

"Thank you, Oscar. I believe I will."

12
What I Know About You

For over twenty years, I have been receiving Truth from Spirit and I like to think that by now, I have learned a thing or two. And so I can say with absolute confidence that I know quite a lot about you. I know about you regardless of your past, what you have done or failed to do and what has been done to you. I know this about you no matter how things are with you now or how you think they will be.

I know this about you:

- You are Spirit, love and light made manifest here on the earth for this time; and when this time is over, you will simply return to pure Spirit
- You are unique in all the universe and, at one and the same time, you are one with all that is; your purpose for this lifetime lies within your uniqueness, but your power to fulfill it lies in the Oneness

- You are here to express your unique being as fully as you can, to shine your light out on the earth and bless us all with your presence
- You are full of power, talent, skill, intelligence, beauty and wonder; everything you need to shine your light is within you
- You are deeply loved and surrounded by guidance; all the help you need to shine your light is around you
- Everything on your path has led you to this moment and you stand exactly where you need to stand in order to take the next step into your shining destiny; you have arrived
- You are reading this book because the time has come for you to take that step.

My mission is to lift as many people up into awareness and light as I can. I believe, I know, that when enough people have reached a certain level of awareness on the earth, the energy on the earth will shift and it will become easier and easier for people to awaken and shine out. Joy and love are infectious and will spread, I know they will.

And when all this happens, when this light and this awareness spread, this Earth craziness will end and this beautiful planet will become the paradise it was always meant to be. And you, you are an important, vital, necessary part of this process.

And of course, the very first light that needs to come on is you. For you are one with all that is and when you heal yourself, when you awaken a new piece of wisdom within you, when you open your heart to love, compassion and forgiveness, then the entire world is healed and we all take one step toward the great shift that is possible.

Oscar and I are about to pull together important information about how to make that shift within yourself. If you are already walking your spiritual path, I hope you will read on to see if there is something wonderful you might have missed in your journeys so far.

And then, please pass on the Earth Survival Guide to everyone you know. For as they shift and heal, we all shift and heal. And the beautiful earth and all the Earthlings upon her will survive another day, to continue to see snow-capped mountains strewn with wildflowers in spring, to sit under palm trees sensually swaying in the ocean breeze, to go through deep mysterious forests full of things that growl and slither, to cross vast open plains full of magnificent roaring beasts.

We owe this to our Mother Earth. We owe this to ourselves.

I believe it can be done. I believe you have the power. In fact, I know this about you.

13
Oscar and Carrie Get to Work

As I finished, Oscar spoke.

"I believe it too, Carrie. And I believe we can compile an Earth Survival Guide that will give Earthlings some of the key understandings they can use to make this happen."

"Yes, Oscar. I agree. And as we go through and create the Guide, let's also put even more resources on www.EarthSurvivalGuideBook.com. We can list websites to visit, books to read and downloadable meditations and energy sessions."

"Excellent. Let's get to work!"

"Did you and The Ancient One discuss where to begin?"

"Yes, we have discussed it at length. The most important thing is this. Humans must, absolutely must, begin to recognize that the voice in their minds is not truth and does not mean them well. They must learn to differentiate between that voice and the truth. They must learn to move toward harmony, love and light and turn away from fear, doubt and worry. When they learn to listen to their own internal truth, they will begin to turn it all around."

"I hope you have some ideas about how to do all that!"

"I do. We do."

I pulled up my document on my computer. "Ready to receive and transcribe," I said. And Oscar began.

"The myths about Adam and Eve are not quite right, you know. Humans were not led astray by knowledge. Knowledge is a wonderful and beautiful thing. They were led astray by fear.

"As you learned yesterday, once in physical form on the Earth, many animals were affected by that strange Earth virus that filled them with a great desire to eat the flesh of other animals. And those infected also developed a great love of the hunt."

Here Oscar paused. I could hear him licking his lips and purring. In my mind, I saw a little flash of Oscar chasing a mouse, as he had been wont to do.

Oh, my, I was sounding like him! His accent was very posh. I might have seen him as one of those Brits in khaki on a safari, with porters carrying the makings for a Pimm's Cup when they arrived at camp.

Oscar sighed and continued.

> *"The humans had a slight infection, which gave them an occasional desire for flesh, but they were also happy with eating plants, and they were living in an area that was filled with bounty, fruits hanging from the trees, just waiting to be picked.*
>
> *"But then, one day, they ventured from their beautiful and safe garden and went walking into the jungle. They heard a sharp cry, a struggle and then silence. They progressed cautiously and silently and peeked around a tree. There was a gigantic tiger devouring its kill. They stepped back carefully, then ran as fast as their feet could carry them, back to safety.*
>
> *"But now they understood that they might be prey for some of the other, larger and more powerful animals and fear struck deep into their hearts. And nothing was ever the same.*

"The humans were very, very smart and that was their tool of survival. They weren't as big and powerful as some animals, but they knew how to build weapons and how to create fires. Like the other animals before them, they adapted. They learned how to survive. A balance was struck among all the animals, including the humans. And life went on.

"But a funny thing happened to the humans. As they reproduced, a strange mutation occurred in their brains. And since this mutation helped them survive in ever-greater numbers, the mutation became a predominant trait in humankind.

"Humans became aware of themselves as mortal beings who exist for a finite amount of time. They began to see everything in terms of the length of time available to them before they died. Unlike the other animals, who exist in the moment, responding to physical threats and instinctively taking action for survival, the human became obsessed with the ideas of death and time.

"The world became deeply threatening and religions and mythology were developed as ways to hold back the terror and seek some form of protection from a cruel world. Ceremonies were created to appease imagined gods. Various forms of wealth were developed as a sophisticated talisman against terror. And what signified wealth was always, by definition, that which was in short supply. Gold and

precious jewels represented wealth precisely because they were rare.

"Since wealth meant safety and protection, and since it was scarce, some humans began to fight with each other to have it. They were deeply afraid when they were without. They learned to fear each other as well as Tiger. And so it was and so it is."

Oscar paused to catch his breath and I did the same. All this was sad, but so, so true. Then he continued.

"The fear and the intelligence both grew and grew. The intelligence had a voice in the mind. It could solve problems effectively. It could even build an airplane and a skyscraper. It was a marvelous tool and it allowed the human to become the predominant power on the Earth.

"But the fear started speaking through that voice too. And the fear didn't have big visions, like airplanes and skyscrapers. The fear only remembered tigers, the finite nature of time and the inevitability of aging and death.

"Fear and his sidekick Doubt believe in scarcity, not abundance. Their job, above all else, is to keep you safe. They believe that all power derives from what is outside you, not what is inside you. And they live and speak in your mind, all the time."

"Yes, Oscar, I know the voices of fear and doubt. They keep me awake at 3 in the morning. Along with the voice of regret."

"Regret is just another form of time-based fear and doubt. Regret says that if only you had done things differently, you would be in a better place now. And the only result of this thinking is to make you even more hesitant about taking courageous action. Because, after all, if you act, you might make a mistake. And then there you'll be, telling yourself all about it at 3 AM."

"You're a pretty smart cat, Oscar!"

"Yes, I was taking a correspondence course at Oxford on your computer while you slept."

"No! Really? Well, I guess it could be. Everything else that's happening is beyond imagining, so why not that?"

"No, not really. Everything I know, I learned from The Ancient One. They don't teach all this at Oxford, in any event."

"You're right about that! And so what did you learn from The Ancient One? What can we do to counteract this voice of fear?"

"The first thing is to realize that the voice of fear masquerades as the voice of reason. It mixes up the really good, productive thinking with the fear and doubt. And so it is highly respected by Earth society, especially at Oxford and Harvard. People forget that the airplane was invented by people who were seen as crazy at the time. And this is always so. People who stare fear and doubt in the face and do what their truth tells them to do, often suffer at the hands of society."

"Until they succeed and get wealth. Then they are revered, worshipped. Then they become celebrities."

"You're a pretty smart cat yourself."

"So what can you tell us about surviving on the Earth, with this mutant voice in our brains?"

"The first thing is to learn to recognize it. And once you recognize it, you know not to trust it. It is lying to you, you know. Not all the time, but enough."

"Lying to me? Isn't that a little strong?"

"Remember the time I disappeared for a few days and you worried that I was hurt or dying? You asked Spirit over and over if I was OK and the answer was always yes. But still you worried. Still that voice said I was dying. It lied."

"Yes. The answer from Spirit was truth, but the voice in my mind was not." I paused for a moment to think. "And by the way, where were you?"

"I was a little ill from the shots the vet gave me, so I was doing what smart cats do. I was lying low without eating until I felt better. I was under the house."

"Ah."

"And years later, when I got sick and truly was dying, what happened then, in your mind?"

"Well, that's interesting. I was very upset, of course, and worried. I didn't want to lose you. But there was also a very calm voice that showed up, a voice of truth and knowing, that simply told me it was time. I knew not to let the vet operate or experiment with drugs. I knew, as much as I didn't want it or like it, that it was time to just let you go. It wasn't that busy voice of worry. It was truth speaking."

> *"Yes, and I thank you for making it easy for me. That was very kind."*

"Oh, Oscar, I miss you so!"

> *"I am right here. There is nothing to miss. Nothing is ever lost."*

"It's not the same as having you here!" I took a deep breath and wiped away my tears. "But you have something you need to tell me, I know. Let's take a little break and then we can continue."

14
Separate Mind

I took several deep breaths and then went outside, remembering Oscar as I strolled around the garden. When the memories were sweet and funny, I returned with a smile, ready to resume our work.

"OK, I'm all right now. Please, what do you have to share?"

"I have put together a list of ways to recognize when the voice in your human mind is not the voice of reason or truth."

"There are so many things we can call that voice. Don Miguel Ruiz, in his wonderful book *The Four Agreements*, calls it both the Judge and the Victim, and I certainly see that. You could also say it's a Protector, but that sounds a little benign. You could say Liar, but it isn't always lying, you just can't know."

"I agree. None of those terms are exactly right. Ruiz comes closest."

"I'm not sure what to call it, but I know what it does. It keeps me suppressed. It keeps me from fully expressing my truth, beauty, intelligence, imagination and talents. It makes me feel on guard and hesitant. It tells me I'm not worthy, that I'm not enough. It tells me not to take a risk, because I'm likely to fail and that failing will be a disaster, not a way to learn and grow. It doesn't want me to be fully alive, vibrantly alive, trying new things, opening my heart and having adventures. It's like a prison guard."

"Except that the prison bars are not real; they are in your mind, created by this voice."

"I've most often heard it called 'Ego' in spiritual circles. But 'Ego' is a little confusing, because Freud made his own use of that term. And there's a common usage, as in 'egotistical,' that isn't quite the same."

We both paused to think.

Suddenly, Oscar brightened. "Separate Mind! That voice believes each human is alone and separate."

"Yes, that is exactly right!"

"And Separate Mind is in contrast to One Mind, which knows it is deeply connected and never

alone, which speaks truth from the center of Spirit and Oneness."

"Perfect! Now, what about this list you made?"

"I documented Eleven Observations, ways to recognize this voice of the Separate Mind, the voice that cannot be trusted, the voice that you should never follow without question."

"How clever! How did you figure it all out?"

"It was nothing, really. Just listening to your thoughts for 14 years!"

"That's scary! Out of the Eleven Observations, which ones seem most important to you?"

"They're all important, but I would choose three as the most critical understandings for people to have."

1. **Separate Mind compares, criticizes and judges. One Mind observes.**

   Whenever you are thinking that this is better than that, or this is wrong and that is right, then you are within Separate Mind. One Mind knows that criticism is a mirror.

2. **Separate Mind lives in the past and future. One Mind lives in the present moment.**
Separate Mind lives in regret for the past and worry over the future and misses the present entirely. When it is not in fear over the future, it may be in grandiose fantasy. One Mind lives now and only now, soaking it all in.

3. **Separate Mind lives in fear and doubt. One Mind thrives on courageous action.**
Separate Mind seeks the familiar. It second-guesses your decisions to move on and try new things. One Mind loves newness and fills you with the courage and confidence to step out bravely into the limitless frontier.

"Oh, that's wonderful, Oscar, but I have so much I want to discuss! I can think of examples in my life for each and every one. And I want to study all Eleven Observations!

"Let's post your Separate Mind observations out on www.EarthSurvivalGuideBook.com, shall we? You and I can have a thorough discussion of all of them there."

> *"That is an excellent idea. I look forward to hearing your examples. Many of them are quite well known to me already, of course."*

"Yes, yes. Who knows what all you saw while lying on my desk. I have some great pictures of you there—and lounging on my computer keyboard! I'll post them on www.EarthSurvivalGuideBook.com too, so that everyone can see how beautiful you were and are."

> *"That would be nice. Hold me in your heart as I hold you in mine."*

"Yes, I will. I do. Good-bye for now."

The transmission was over and the demands of the ordinary day were upon me. A day in which to review the taxes from the accountant and figure out how in the world I was going to pay them. I spent the day searching for additional deductions and finding none. How had I managed to underestimate the taxes so badly? What was I going to do now?

Finally I went to bed. After some tossing and turning, I managed to go to sleep.

15
Flutterby Teaches Me to Reach Silence

I awoke at 3 AM, the dreaded worry hour, and all I could think about were those taxes. My mind was in an endless obsessive loop.

Oscar was certainly right about Separate Mind living in the past and future. Here I was torturing myself with worry, when, in fact, right now, in the present moment, I was just lying in my comfortable bed. It was fear of the future and regret for the past that had me obsessing.

Suddenly, a butterfly landed on my nose! And what a butterfly. Absolutely gorgeous, with various shades of purple, turquoise and green. But on my nose, fluttering away!

"Who are you and what are you doing?" I asked.

But she was not much of a talker, this one. She just fluttered on my nose, then flew toward the bedroom door and waited. When I didn't respond, she returned to my nose.

Again, no speaking. Perhaps she was like a faerie, who only whispers. I listened very hard, but she just flew again to the door.

I sighed and rubbed my eyes. Feeling rather grumpy, I wrapped my robe around myself and went to the door.

Instantly, she was off to the back door. So I opened it and we both went outside into the garden. There was a full moon shining down upon us, lighting up the garden in the most magical way. The butterfly went right to my bench, the stone bench with a white azaleas wrapped around it, the one where I had first met my Spirit Guide, Quado.

I sat down on the bench and instantly felt more peaceful and centered. She fluttered right next to my ear. Finally, I heard a tiny little high-pitched whisper.

"Would you like to know how to quiet your mind?"

"Yes, that would be great. Thank you. And by the way, are you sent by The Ancient One?"

"Yes. I am Flutterby Butterfly."

"Very nice to meet you. Yes, I would love to know how to quiet my mind."

"You must trick your mind by asking it a question that can only be answered by your body."

FLUTTERBY TEACHES ME TO REACH SILENCE

That wasn't particularly useful, actually.

"How?" I asked. She gave a little flutter as if to say, these humans are not very bright! But then she whispered the answer.

"Close your eyes and take 3 deep breaths."

Ah, that was nice. I felt better already. Why did I so often forget to breathe?

"Then hold one hand up so that it is not touching anything."

I bent my right arm at the elbow, with my hand in the air.

She fluttered her approval and then continued. "Now ask your mind this question: How do I know my hand exists?"

I did as she asked. And something amazing happened. The noise and energy instantly left my busy mind and flew to my hand. It was answering my question the only way it could. I couldn't see my hand, because my eyes were closed. I couldn't feel my hand, because it wasn't touching anything. So the answer had to be supplied by attention and energy.

And the truly beautiful thing was that my mind had gone completely silent; for one blessed moment, I wasn't thinking. The mutant human brain was still. What a relief!

Now I brought up my other hand, still with my eyes closed. I asked the question again and as before, the energy flew to my hand. I then discovered that when my mind started its inevitable chatting again, I could just ask the question, and for some reason, my mind felt compelled to answer it, over and over. And each time, I was given the gift of silence, a silence that seemed to be lasting longer and longer.

"Thank you Ms. Flutterby Butterfly! You have given me a priceless gift. I thank you."

And with that, she just made a little dip, as if to say "You're welcome!" and disappeared from my life, fluttering away into the moonlit night.

How to Quickly Quiet Your Mind

1. Close your eyes.
2. Breathe deeply three times.
3. Hold one hand up, so that it is not touching anything. Just bending your elbow is an excellent way to do this, since it leaves your hand supported.
4. Ask this question, silently in your mind: How do I know my hand exists?
5. If you wish, lift up the other hand and ask again.
6. If your mind begins to chatter, ask again.

FLUTTERBY TEACHES ME TO REACH SILENCE

I sat there for a moment enjoying the way my thoughts were stretched out and the silence could be heard between them. The obsessive thoughts were gone completely. This is the goal of meditation, to reach this silence. And here I was, sitting outside on a balmy night with moonlight streaming down upon me. Truly One Mind, living in the present moment. More meditation seemed like a lovely idea.

I knew that if I did meditate for a while, I would increase my chances of coming up with a great solution to my tax issue. Or at the very least, I would accept the situation more peacefully.

I decided to do a simple mantra meditation, using 'So Hum," the Sanskrit for 'I am that.'

I lay down on the soft grass. Yes, I know, some people say you should always sit up to meditate. But they just have a problem with falling asleep during meditation, something that had never happened to me. And there is something about lying on the grass under a bright moon that is beyond magical.

I closed my eyes and mentally watched my breath, coming in, filling me, and leaving. As I watched it come in, I silently said "So." As I watched it depart, I silently said "Hum." And that was it. Softly and gently, letting thoughts pass through on their way to nowhere, just seeking the silence between them and watching it stretch out further and further.

How to Do a Simple Mantra Meditation

1. Set a soothing timer for 20 minutes or so.

2. Sit comfortably and close your eyes.

3. Begin to watch your breath entering and leaving your body. If visualization is difficult for you, then just feel your breath or simply focus on the mantra.

4. Do not try to change your breathing in any way. Just breathe normally.

5. As you inhale, watch the breath come in and silently say "So" in your mind.

6. As you exhale, watch the breath leave and silently say "Hum" in your mind.

7. If your mind wanders, and it probably will, just let the thoughts float through and then resume your mantra. Don't worry; it is perfectly normal.

8. When your timer goes off, slowly return, wiggling your fingers and toes. Then congratulate yourself for having done the exercise. Even if your mind was busy, you have gained the many benefits of meditation simply by doing it.

16
Power Animals Revisited

I guess I must have fallen asleep—even though I NEVER do that when meditating—because the next thing I knew, there was a very familiar, very loud purr in my ear, and a British-accented voice saying:

> "Aren't you going to do your morning i-am-this.com Empowerment? I'm slated to talk to you after you finish, so you really do need to begin!"

I was so startled. I looked around and realized I was out in the garden lying on the lawn. What in the world? Then I remembered Flutterby and smiled. Ah, beautiful Flutterby Butterfly. What a gift she had given me.

"Wake up, wake up now!"

"Oscar. This reminds me of how you would walk across my head when you wanted to go out at 3

AM. And knock books off the nightstand if I didn't get up right away."

"Ah, yes. I enjoyed that bit, watching you jump as the books hit the floor. But being able to talk and wake you up this way is even better!"

"I even miss that about you."

"It's time to get up, Carrie. The Empowerment call is due to start."

I jumped up and went inside, where I found that I had only one minute to get going.

"Thank you, Oscar," I called as I rushed into my office and started dialing into the call.

After a lovely Empowerment, I found that Oscar was right there waiting.

"What's up, Oscar?"

"Our job today is to update the Power Animal Retrieval techniques, so that people can do them on their own. We can no longer wait for the Shaman community to regain the power to do this for everyone. People need to learn on their own that this great source of personal power belongs to them, whenever they need it."

"Very good. I have some thoughts, though, that I would like to discuss first."

"By all means."

"From what I've studied, things written by anthropologists who have lived in societies that still have active shamans, a sick or unhappy person is one without a power animal. They can be healed and made whole by retrieving a power animal and joining with its power. And it is up to them to keep that animal happy, by doing the things that will please it. Running like a gazelle, for example."

Oscar nodded. This was his understanding as well.

"And from this view, the essential, central power and health of a person is derived from the presence of the power animal."

Oscar gave a big cat yawn.

"But I don't really believe that's true."

Oscar perked up. "No? What do you believe?"

"It's like what we discussed earlier. I believe that all power is already inside each person. I think that people dilute their power through their emotions and thoughts, but that the ability to retrieve and exercise their power lies within them."

"Like what you said in your 'What I Know About You' section."

"Yes, just like that. And I think the Power Animal concept as it is handed down from those older cultures needs some updating, if it is to be useful to people who are alive now."

"Please continue. What do you see?"

"Funny you should put it that way. What do I see? Many years ago I did see something, a vision in my mind's eye. And it has held up very well."

"Please share."

17
Carrie's Vision

I took a deep breath and then brought my vision forth to look at as I spoke. Even after all these years, I could see so vividly what I had experienced one day in my garden.

"I saw a shadowy region where we all live. And above that region—or dimension, or level, whatever you want to call it—was another region, which contained big, bright shining lights, which were our souls or higher selves. And above that was the highest level, which was complete light. You could call that highest level The Great All, Source or Oneness."

"Or God."

"Yes, or God. And at the lowest level, in the shadows, were the people, like me. There was a cord that ran from the top of each person's head up to a bright shining light in the soul level. I saw that most people had some light flowing down this cord, but it was somewhat clogged or twisted, allowing only partial light to flow. A few, especially those in deep meditation, had a lovely open, golden flow, coming right from Soul that just lit them up. They were so beautiful and glowing. And a few lost and unhappy people had very twisted cords and were receiving almost no light at all."

"And the Power Animals?"

"In that shadowy land full of lost and stumbling people, there were some glowing lights that were not people. They were spiritual entities who had chosen to come down from the higher regions to help humankind. They were there among the humans speaking to them, guiding and assisting. And some people paid attention and some did not.

"Some of them were what we call spirit guides, some were angels, some were masters and some were power animals. It's difficult to say what all there may be. I think that what surrounds a particular person may be related to what it is that they can accept, what they might be most open to."

"What has been your experience, about the entities and what they offer?"

CARRIE'S VISION

"My personal spiritual awakening was through a spirit guide, Quado. He taught me the basic spiritual truths and was also my close friend when I needed one. So my view of a spirit guide is one who provides deep wisdom as well as advice on daily matters and decisions."

"Any personal experience with angels and archangels?"

"I've had a lot of experience with angels. In my view, they have been very practical assistants. They help clear heavy burdens of the past and they actually take action to assist you in achieving important things in your life, like telling you what to read, which way to turn and introducing you to the people who open opportunities. The tricky part about angels, though, is that you have to ask for their help. If you don't ask, they just sit around, bored and waiting."

"They're bored?"

I laughed. "Well, I say that only because of one experience I had. I was once procrastinating about doing something difficult, and when I finally acted, I saw a group of angels toss down the magazines they were reading, get up from couches and easy chairs and say: 'Well, finally! At last she'd going to do something!"

"And to think I didn't even know they read magazines! And Power Animals?"

"I believe Power Animals offer invaluable emotional support. And since most illness is caused by emotions that are out of balance, they can also have a strong effect on health, just as the ancient shamans believed. When you bring in their emotional stability and their ability to live in the present moment, you have taken a great step forward in dealing with life on Earth, which is no small feat!"

"Do you have a Power Animal?"

"In these times, I would like people to think of Power Animals in two ways. One way is a totem animal that is your primary support and companion, which is probably what you meant."

"Yes, that's correct."

"I would encourage people to have a Power Animal Team, not just one. It's a complex world we live in!"

"Who's on your team?"

"Since I was a child playing Jungle, I have always connected with Panther. Something about that silent, patient watchfulness and readiness. But there are times I have pulled in Tiger, who is more proactive and great for tackling big projects. I think they both exist within me, each becoming more dominant as required.

"But here's the really important thing I wanted to convey. As much as I love having my basic Power Animal Team always right there and helping to stabilize me and keep me company, I am beginning to think that the most important use of Power Animals is in bringing them in as archetypes for specific situations and relationships. Maybe it's because our crazy society is just so demanding and requires us to be so many different things. But I really think it's an incredibly useful skill, to know how to bring them in quickly and as needed."

"What do you mean by bringing them in as archetypes?"

"What I mean is that you can bring them in as a form of concentrated energy with specific characteristics, without necessarily getting to know them deeply and personally. Their power as archetypes is derived greatly from your mental and emotional associations with them, as well as what they are actually bringing.

"A great example is Lion. We associate Lion with presence, dignity, courage and confidence. When you breathe in Lion as archetype, you are bringing to yourself those characteristics, without concerning yourself with this particular lion's name or personality, as you might with a lifetime totem animal.

"You simply breathe Lion power into your heart and then walk into that intimidating meeting with all that courage and confidence within you. And when challenged, you take a deep breath and refresh Lion in your heart before speaking."

"That sounds excellent. Do you have specific instructions for doing this?"

"I do."

18
Inviting Power Animal Archetypes

Here's how to invite a Power Animal Archetype to fill you with power :

1. Plan to give yourself 5 minutes or so to prepare before your challenging event. Bring in the power just before you need it.
2. Find a quiet place where you can be alone, possibly your car or the restroom. With time, you can learn to do this quickly wherever you are.
3. Close your eyes and breathe deeply, breathing down to a receptive state.
4. If you know the right Power Animal, then picture him or her.
5. If you're uncertain, ask for the right Power Animal to appear in your mind's eye
6. Say hello. Ask if he or she would be kind enough to be within you. (They always say yes!). Give your thanks.
7. Now, holding the picture in your mind, breathe in your Power Animal in three deep breaths. Each time, see the animal entering on your

breath as you inhale and feel the power filling and expanding within you on the exhale.
8. If possible, extend your arms; show your wings or your claws. Give a roar! (Not recommended in all circumstances.)
9. Fill yourself with confidence and courage. Breathe! Roar! Leap! Fly!
10. When it is time, stand up, pull your shoulders back and chest forward. Lift your chin. Carry yourself like the magnificent beast you are! You can do it!
11. If you need to, during the event, just breathe in your power animal again and again. When you speak, speak truth with confidence and presence. Don't be afraid to pause in a meaningful way before speaking—it gives you a chance to reconnect and gives you an air of gravitas as well.

"What do you think Oscar?"

"You said to breathe down to a receptive state. What if someone is too nervous?"

"You're right. It is something that may require some practice. Luckily, I have a technique to recommend!

19
How to Breathe Down

When I first started talking to Spirit, it was difficult for me to come down out of my habitually tense state. I practiced the technique below every morning, until my body knew a new way to be. Then I was able to calm myself no matter what.

1. If you can, go to the same place every day at the same time to practice. Your body will begin to take the location and time as a cue to relax. Consider giving yourself an extra cue, like touching your thumb to your index or middle finger. That might come in handy when you are in other physical surroundings.
2. Close your eyes.
3. Inhale deeply and silently begin to count, beginning with "ten, ten, ten."
4. As you exhale, repeat "ten, ten, ten."
5. Now inhale and silently say "nine, nine, nine."
6. Repeat as you exhale, "nine, nine, nine."

7. Continue until you reach One. If you are still tense, begin again at ten.
8. When you reach that deeply relaxed state, note what it feels like. You may feel tingly, floaty or both. It is a specific state in your body, a specific brain frequency, which you will begin to recognize. The more you practice, the easier it is to slip right into this state in 3 deep breaths.
9. You are now in the place where magic occurs, where you may invite power animals, angels and spirit guides to come forth and assist. This is also where you have direct access to your intuitive senses. Just relax and do not push. Gentle, gentle is the way.

20
Power Animal Team

Oscar did some deep breathing himself, and then continued.

"Excellent. What are some power animals that work well as Archetypes in the ways of today's world?"

"The success of the archetype approach depends upon each person's perception of what a particular power animal represents, and so it may vary from person to person. But here are a few that may form the foundation of a Power Animal Team for most people."

LION

Circumstance: Public speaking, meeting with higher-status people

Conveys: I have presence, dignity, confidence and courage. Even my silence speaks eloquently of my power.

How to Act: Hold your head high. Pause before speaking. Speak at a measured pace and with a lower tone. Speak from your deep center of truth.

LIONESS

Circumstance: Motivating a team to do something challenging

Conveys: I get down to business. I am the master of efficient, no-nonsense, successful action

How to Act: Look directly in the eyes when speaking. Share a vision of the objective. Convey certainty of success. Be clear about action to be taken.

LEOPARD

Circumstance: Uncertain setting and unknown people

Conveys: I'm not seen until I want to be noticed — and then I am something to behold!

How to Act: Be very quiet. Listen and watch from your perch. When you are ready, jump down off the bough and shine forth with your beauty!

RHINOCEROS

Circumstance: Difficult and unpredictable meeting, possibly threatening, such as meeting with an ex

Conveys: You can come this far, but no further. I am listening, but I'm not a pushover. There are limits to what I allow. I am not disturbed by small annoyances.

How to Act: Listen more and speak less. No smiling, apologies or nervous laughter. Absolute composure and fearlessness. Eyes direct but noncommittal. If you must charge, do it full out with rhino power.

SEAGULL

Circumstance: Alone and in peace

Conveys: I soar in freedom and joy

How to Act: At last, a moment alone, to dip into the present moment and remember that you are a bird and can fly! Glide on the wind. Fly over the waves. Call out to the world: I am, I am!

SWAN

Circumstance: Formal and elegant setting

Conveys: I belong here. I am graceful and tasteful. I set the standard for beauty and manners. I am completely secure.

How to Act: Act with absolute confidence, knowing that you can do no wrong. Be gracious and complimentary, going out of your way to make everyone feel as admired as you know you are.

SQUIRREL

Circumstance: Meeting with the tax accountant, banker or auditor

Conveys: I know who I am. I balance savings and practicality with joy and abandon. I may be running a little short of nuts right now, but I will survive the winter and am not afraid.

How to Act: Be relaxed and confident. Stay calm no matter what. Later, remember to laugh at life.

TIGER

Circumstance: Big project you must complete or territory you must protect

Conveys: I just do it, with tireless energy. I patrol my territory and challenge all comers. I get it done no matter what.

How to Act: Relax and know Tiger is on it. Try your best to enjoy the process, while knowing that success is yours.

GIRAFFE

Circumstance: Social situation around intimidatingly beautiful people or meeting with the ex's newbie

Conveys: I am perfect. I love how I look and who I am. I love being uniquely me.

How to Act: Relax. No fussing with clothes or hair. Not a care in the world. Casual and nonchalant.

BUFFALO

Circumstance: Worse than you ever imagined

Conveys: I endure. No wind is too strong, no snow too heavy, to stop me. I live for another day.

How to Act: Listen more and speak less. When you can, howl out your pain and then pull yourself together. The spring always comes, always. No winter lasts forever.

BEAR

Circumstance: Feeling as if you could really, really use a hug

Conveys: I love myself! My deep and lasting affection extends to me.

How to Act: Confident and well-loved, smiling and warm, affectionate and caring. Reach out and touch someone!

EAGLE

Circumstance: Time to step forward and lead

Conveys: I have greatness within me. I am completely comfortable in a leadership role and having others look to me for solutions. I soar above the problems and have perspective.

How to Act: Absolutely confident, as if you have been a leader for life. Step out of the details and into the vision. Assign others to do the detail work as you show the way.

FOX

Circumstance: Room full of people you don't know who seem to know each other

Conveys: I am easy and relaxed with people, because I know I am infinitely charming!

How to Act: Smile, relax. You own the room. Let them do all the talking and they'll find you fascinating.

GORILLA

Circumstance: Meeting with intimidating people where you must make a strong impression

Conveys: I can pound my chest because you and I both know how strong and powerful I am.

How to Act: Forget all your training about deference and not showing off. Speak up! Say what you know!

PANTHER

Circumstance: Waiting, waiting

Conveys: I have all the time in the world. I wait up here on my bough until just the right moment and then I pounce.

How to Act: Relaxed and patient. Facial expression alert and aware. Body relaxed, but attentive and ready.

UNICORN

Circumstance: I could really use a miracle about now

Conveys: I am faith and mystery. My energy has power. I project what I desire, fully, from the glowing light in my center. Limitless possibilities abound.

How to Act: Deeply peaceful and yet powerful, with a strength that emanates from your solar plexus. You light up the world with the strength of your belief.

It was fun to talk about my Power Animal friends. They have been such a gift to me!

"I can see that some of these power animals could be useful companions for long stretches. Can they be used that way as well?"

"Yes. To form your basic power animal team, you may either just identify them by feel and invite them to be within you, or you may hold a Power Animal Retrieval. It would be wonderful if we knew the best way for someone to do this on their own, if they don't have access to a shaman. It would be so great if everyone could have a power animal team."

"Let's take a break. I will consult with The Ancient One in the Land of Ur."

"Excellent. I will see you tomorrow, then."

21
Power Animal Retrieval

The next morning, Oscar was right there as I finished up the Empowerment.

"The Ancient One agrees with you, Carrie These are do-it-yourself times, and humans should be able to come to the Land of Ur on their own, if they choose.

"The power animals in Ur have been alerted to expect humans to be wandering around, seeking help. We will be watching for them. Here's what they need to do."

How to Retrieve Your Power Animal

1. Determine how you will reach the Land of Ur. You could enter a cave, jump into a pool of water, slide down the root of a tree, or hop into a hole. (For clarity: this is a journey you will make in your mind, so choose anything you like!)

2. If you prefer, you may go into the cave of my shaman, Running Wolf, and ask his assistance. Or you may ask Spirit to introduce you to another shaman.
3. Determine how you will bring yourself into a deep meditative state. Playing a recording of shaman drumming is highly recommended, but deep breathing alone could also work.
4. Get comfortable and close your eyes.
5. Breathe or drum yourself down to a receptive state.
6. Enter the earth as you had decided. But if Spirit shows you a different way, take it.
7. After you enter, you will begin to tumble down a passageway, like a rabbit hole. Just let yourself tumble and tumble, until you finally tumble out.
8. Look around. You might tumble onto a shoreline or deep within the ocean. You might tumble out into a rainforest or jungle. You might be on the African Serengeti, the Great American Plains or the North Pole. Whatever it is, accept it, live it, let it be. You are there, in the Land of Ur.
9. Walk or swim forward. Just keep going and let it come to you.

POWER ANIMAL RETRIEVAL

10. If an animal presents itself to you in four aspects, like front, back, side and side, it means that he or she is offering to be your Power Animal.
11. Reach out and pull the Power Animal to your heart. At this point, you might be returned to where you were before going to the Land of Ur. Just continue wherever you find yourself.
12. Thank your Power Animal for being within you, for coming into your life to be your companion and helper.
13. If you care to, you may ask your power animal his or her name. If you don't receive an answer now, don't worry. The name will come to you later, perhaps when you least expect it.
14. Now, you may perform a ceremony to welcome your power animal. Perhaps you could light a candle and sing a song of joy and welcome as you invite your new companion to be within you. If you have chosen to have a Spirit shaman assist you, she will blow the power animal essence into your heart and the crown of your head. At the conclusion of your ceremony, you may say: We are now one.
15. You might wish to have reminders of your power animal with you. Perhaps you could

create a little altar or wear jewelry with his or her image.
16. Before you go into stressful situations, spend a moment preparing with your power animal. Breathe deeply. Pull in the energy. Your power animal is there to help you stay true and stay within your power. Use the power that is there for you!
17. And when you have a moment, go outside and walk or run, swim or fly. Both you and your power animal will love it!

"I'm so glad we have this tool to offer. Sometimes I think that this highly complex society that we have come up with is much more than people are equipped to handle, emotionally."

"For myself, I was always pleased to be a cat who didn't have to deal with it all."

"I have often wished I could just be a cat, well-fed as you were, snoozing away."

"Ah, if only you knew the energy I expended on your behalf!"

"I think perhaps I do. Thank you, Oscar. And now, I need to return to my taxes."

"Perhaps Squirrel will give you a hand."

"Perhaps. Or Fox, to help me be very clever. Or Coyote, to make me wily."

"Or Unicorn, to help you stay true while opening to magic and possibility."

"Ah, yes, of course. I will call in Unicorn."

After Oscar left, I sat down at my desk. I opened up all my intuitive receptors. I pictured my beautiful Unicorn friend and breathed her in, asking her to be with me with her magical powers while I looked once more at the taxes.

I tried to open the drawer with the tax materials. It was stuck. I tugged and pulled, finally pulling the entire drawer out of the desk and nearly falling over backwards in the process. And then I blinked in amazement. There, in the spot where the drawer had been, was a folder of receipts I had missed.

It had fallen back behind the drawer and slid underneath.

I gave my thanks to Unicorn and got to work. Whew. I was saved!

22
Intuition

I awoke the next morning feeling rested and ready. After the morning Empowerment, I just sat quietly and waited, and sure enough, Oscar popped into my mind.

"Good morning, Carrie. Did you sleep well?"

"I slept very well, thanks to Unicorn's help. I'm all set to go with our next topic."

"Your thoughts?"

"An Earth Survival Guide wouldn't be complete without knowing how to make good use of our natural intuition."

"Other animals quite naturally survive on instinct and intuition, but the human tribe is so busy listening to the busy, mutant mind, that it has lost touch with this most important sense."

"You will get no argument from me. These terms like Paranormal, Extra Sensory Perception, Psychic and Mind Reading all make it sound as if it is a weird subset of human society that has a special power, one to be feared. But the fact is, everyone has these senses. They are just as natural in the human body as the physical senses."

"Yes, I watch people as they quite naturally use the gift. They sense how others feel about them, energetically, intuitively. They suddenly know who is calling before they answer the phone. They run in and check on the baby just in time. They open the big book right to the answer they are seeking."

"And of course, over and over, they smack themselves on the forehead and say 'I knew I shouldn't have done that!' Because, once again, they ignored their natural intuition.

"It is tricky, though, because even though intuition gives you knowledge of what is happening now and what is likely to happen in the future, if you were to listen to all of that, all the time, it would be overwhelming. So we filter it out.

"Sometimes I wish that intuition would be louder, not just a whisper."

"Sometimes it is."

"True. When it is vitally important, it can be very strong indeed. I know that one of the best ways to control the filtering is with attention. If you study, observe and pay attention to some area of your life, you begin to get intuitive information about it. If you deny it and turn away in fear and doubt, your intuitive filter closes down."

> "Yes, and so denying the existence of intuition can be something of a self-fulfilling prophecy. Those who say it doesn't exist are likely receiving less intuitive information in their lives than someone who is open and receptive."

"Just like love."

> "Indeed. Intuition is such an important topic to you, Carrie. What do you want to include in the Earth Survival Guide?"

"It's so important, but such a big topic. I think I'd like to say just a little here, about how to recognize intuition, and then put a fuller explanation of the intuitive senses and how to use and enhance them out on www.EarthSurvivalGuideBook.com. Then those who care to study more deeply can do so."

> "Excellent. I am all ears."

"I first learned about intuition by looking at it as four intuitive senses: Feeling, Seeing, Hearing and Knowing. So I think I'll say a bit about each of these and how they manifest in our ordinary, daily lives."

"Very good. How do you understand the sense of feeling?"

"A Feeler is very sensitive to the energy of others. She can walk into the room and feel the emotions of the people within it. She is highly empathic; she truly does know how someone else feels. It's a very handy sense to have as a therapist or coach, but it can be overwhelming."

"Any advice for the Feeler?"

"Yes. Use your empathy as a tool, but learn to recognize when the feeling does not belong to you. When you are alone, practice centering yourself and knowing what it feels like to be you. Then when you are with a strongly projecting person, learn to say, 'This is not mine' and allow it to flow through and out."

"Hearing?"

"I am using my sense of intuitive hearing right now, in listening to you. It's how I receive messages from Spirit."

"How does it sound to you?"

"Good question. It's internal. It sounds like my own thinking, but has a different feel somehow and is located in a different place in my head. My own thinking is usually on one side or the other. When I am hearing intuitively, it's right in the middle of my head.

"Of course, the main way I can tell the difference between my so-called rational thinking and intuitive hearing is in the content. My intuition speaks from One Mind. My own thinking is from ego and Separate Mind."

"Ah, of course. How about Seeing?"

"There are several ways this sense appears. Some people see physical energy, like auras. Some people have lucid dreams. Some have visions.

"For me, some things appear brighter when my intuition wants me to notice them. If I find my eye and attention suddenly drawn to one book on the shelf, I will often find that the title of the book is a message for me. Or I might be drawn to a magazine article that holds an answer I was seeking."

"Is there a difference between visualizing and receiving a vision?"

"Oh, you ask just the right questions! There is a slightly different quality to the picture. When I visualize and am projecting the picture from my own thoughts, it is clear. When I am receiving a vision, it is a little grainier sometimes and not very detailed, like an impressionistic painting.

"And when I am speaking to Spirit in my Empowerments, using my sense of intuitive hearing, I am also seeing what I speak of. I am actually using all of my intuitive senses at once."

"How about Knowing?"

"I love this sense! You just know. Sometimes it's little things that come in a flash, like who is on the phone before you pick it up. But sometimes it's a big knowing, a knowing of what important decision you need to make, what direction your life should take. And sometimes it's so strong. All the rational reasons in the world can't hold a candle to that feeling of just knowing the right thing to do."

"Any hints for the Knower?"

"Yes. Trust. Learn to trust your knowing. You will be surprised at the authority it carries if you just present it straight out. When you say, 'I know this is the right direction,' people listen. They can feel the truth and authority within it as well."

INTUITION

"*Intuition is a big topic.*"

"A lifetime study, actually. But I can start people on the path of learning and experimentation, if they'll go out to www.EarthSurvivalGuideBook.com.

"You need to experiment, because, as with the physical senses, everyone is unique in their natural intuitive abilities. I believe everyone has most of the intuitive senses to some extent, but some may be like having 20/20 vision and some may be fuzzy and unclear. I always tell people to experiment and if they find that one intuitive sense doesn't work well, just try another."

"*I agree completely. Everyone is trained in Earthling school to push hard and to focus on learning what is hardest for them, but people need to do the opposite with intuitive senses. They are like wild animals in the forest that will come to you when you are quiet, still and infinitely patient.*"

"Easy for a cat to say. You can sit and wait for a mouse for hours."

"*Most species are more patient than humans! Is there anything else you want to say about intuition here?*"

"I've found that one good way to approach this exploration is to keep an Intuition Journal. Every morning, you practice your intuitive skills and write down the results.

"It's great to keep a journal, because intuition is so subtle. You can write down the results of the morning exercises and then at the end of the day, write down how your intuition spoke to you during the day, hunches you received, anything that just felt possibly intuitive. Over time, you will begin to see patterns emerging."

"You mentioned morning exercises…"

"Oh, right. I'll put them out on the website. Practicing, on your own and with a friend, is the very best way to enhance and expand your intuitive senses.

"You see, no one else can really teach you how this will work best for you. You can listen to other people, but accept only what feels right, what takes you into your own unique gifts. With intuition, you own your own education.

"I always tell people: Value your uniqueness. Know that there are no mistakes, only learning and growing. Welcome to a world where you are full of power, your own power!

"And not just for learning intuition!"

"Too true. I've also found that meditations, including my shamanic Empowerments, heighten the intuitive senses. But as a person living in this Earth-bound human body, I know how difficult it can be, especially at first, to get to a deep place where you can easily access your intuition. Regular meditation and Empowerments help train you, but you also need to learn to breathe."

"Yes, yes. Breathing down to a receptive state, as we covered earlier. Counting from ten to one until it comes easily and naturally."

"That was how I learned to access my intuition. Which led me to Quado. Which opened all the doors to the next twenty years of spiritual exploration.

"And now I do have one last thought for the readers of our Survival Guide."

"By all means."

"Just as it is not necessary to understand electricity in order to learn to turn on the lights so you can see at night, it is not necessary to understand why intuition works in order to learn to turn it on at will and take advantage of the vast storehouse of information available to you."

"And in your experience, what kind of information can you receive this way?"

"Oh, there's so much. It seems to take so many things into account: What others are doing and thinking; the likely outcome of events planned and underway; and our own desires for our future. The answers are all there if we will simply go into the present moment and ask: What shall I do now?"

"Definitely the right question to ask. And now, my intuition says it's time for a nap!"

23

Spirit Songs

The next morning, instead of my usual Empowerment, which usually involves a lot of speaking in English, I found myself singing in a language I did not understand. I couldn't say exactly what the words were saying, but they clearly had meaning and resonated with a very deep truth. In fact, it all felt deeper into Spirit than I had ever gone before.

When I finished, I heard the calm, true voice of The Ancient One.

"Beautiful, Carrie."

"Thank goodness you are here. What was I saying? And in what language?"

"You sang and spoke in the language of Spirit. And what you said cannot be translated. Your earth languages, like English, do not have the words to convey it. Yet it is the closest to pure truth you have ever come."

"Yes. I felt it resonating at a very deep level. There is some level at which I do understand it."

"That is true. And that is why you must continue to receive and share these Spirit songs. Deep inside the human heart, they are heard and understood. And they convey deeply important messages, messages that humans must heed if you are to save yourselves and this planet."

"Oh my. What now? It feels as if a new adventure is beginning. A new door is opening and I must go walk through."

"Indeed."

"But what about the Earth Survival Guide? Do I need to follow this new direction first in order to finish this guide?"

"Not at all. You and Oscar have written quite enough. The most important thing right now is for people to learn the difference between the false voice of Separate Mind and the truth of One Mind that lies within. The answers are all inside, once you know how to hear truth."

"And I can continue to put things out on www.EarthSurvivalGuideBook.com , like some of the wise and wonderful Empowerments that I have received over the years."

SPIRIT SONGS

"Yes. And you will also point to the new directions you are heading."

"The Spirit Singing feels vitally important. I feel that I am carrying forth a resonance that is essential to be shared."

"And so it is. Vitally important. You are not only delivering messages, but you are releasing transformational energies upon the earth as you sing, energies that will allow people to lift to new levels and dimensions.

"But it is also important to share the Earth Survival Guide that you and Oscar have written."

"Where is Oscar? If our work is done, then I need to say good-bye!"

"I am here, Carrie."

"Oscar!"

"I am here in your heart and mind. Always."

"Yes, of course. Thank you for coming by to remind me. I know, nothing is ever lost, not really. I will be talking to you soon, then."

"As often as you like."

And with that, our job was done.

24
It's All About You

Before I go, I have one last experience to share.

Just yesterday, I suddenly felt an enormous opening, an energetic portal with a great, fresh breeze blowing through. And I felt and saw a great financial revival of the American middle class, with abundance and freedom for many, lying just ahead.

And then I saw that women will lead the way. Women stepping into truth and inner power, creative and free, not imitating old ways and trying to fit into old hierarchies, but moving as women can and do, with connection, community and above all, love.

And of course, right beside them, holding hands in the circle of life, were the men who can also see that the old ways must end as we drink of the milk of human kindness and remember who we truly are.

And so, to those of you who feel as if you have been on the fringes of society, locked out of the storehouses of prosperity, I say this. It is time, past time, to set aside your fear, hesitation and self-doubt. It is time to recognize that the feelings of low self-worth and I'm-not-enough, were simply caused by our society and are not your truth, not at all.

It is time to absolutely know that everything you need is inside you. You are full of talents, skills and creativity that want to blossom forth in uniqueness. You are unique, original, one of a kind. There is no one in the entire universe who can bring forth exactly the wonder that you have within you. And the full expression of this unique inner power is your purpose. It is the reason you are here, to shine forth with all that you have and let your light grace the earth.

Will this take courage? Yes, it will!

Can you do it? Yes, you can!

Will you need to open to new ways of being, dig deep within that well of truth and bring forward aspects of yourself that have not yet been admired and appreciated? Will you need to learn to speak your truth in spite of indifference or criticism? Quite probably, yes. But you can do this.

Will you need to simply be who you are, fully expressing your beauty, truth and wonder in everything you do and say? Yes, please. Right now. Yes, please.

IT'S ALL ABOUT YOU

And now, I hand it over to you. Practice learning to hear One Mind. Practice utilizing your great, natural gift of intuition, which helps you hear One Mind more clearly. Remember always that you are deeply loved and surrounded by help and guidance.

Ask. Ask for what you need in order to shine. Ask other people to help you. Ask your wonderful helpers, including angels, spirit guides and power animals.

You are worth the helping. You are important. You matter. There is a place for you in this life. There are people looking for someone just like you, if only you will shine out and let them find you.

The key to survival on earth is really that simple: Be who you truly are.

ABOUT THE AUTHOR

Carrie Hart is a Spiritual Pathfinder, author, inspirational speaker and singer/songwriter.

Since 1999, she has invited others to join her spiritual journey via her unique websites, and her varied and changing offerings in support of our deepest inner journey.

Go to www.EarthSurvivalGuideBook.com for links to her current websites and programs, as well as free downloads and resources to help you on the journey outlined in this book.

www.ingramcontent.com/pod-product-compliance
Lightning Source LLC
Chambersburg PA
CBHW051650040426
42446CB00009B/1068